THE MITCHELL BEAZLEY POCKET GUIDE TO

Garden Birds

Dominic Couzens
& Mike Langman

ACKNOWLEDGEMENTS

Dominic Couzens would like to thank all those who contributed their help during the preparation of this book, especially the members of the London and Surrey adult education classes.

USEFUL ADDRESSES

• British Trust for Ornithology, National Centre for Ornithology, The Nunnery, Thetford, Norfolk IP24 2PU (01842 750050)
• Royal Society for the Protection of Birds, (RSPB), The Lodge, Sandy, Bedfordshire SG19 2DL (01767 680551)
• C J Wildbird Foods Ltd, The Rea, Upton Magna, Shrewsbury SY4 4UB (01743 709545)

RECOMMENDED READING AND LISTENING

• *Bird Watching*, Bretton Court, Bretton, Peterborough PE3 8DZ. Available on subscription or from newsagents.
• *The Birdfeeder Handbook* by Robert Burton. RSPB/Dorling Kindersley.
• *The Bird Table Book* by Tony Soper. David and Charles.
• *Teach Yourself Bird Sounds*, No 1. Garden Birds. Waxwing Associates, Little Okeford House, Christchurch Road, Tring, Hertfordshire HP23 4EF

First published in 1996 by Mitchell Beazley,
an imprint of Reed Consumer Books Limited
Michelin House, 81 Fulham Road,
London SW3 6RB, and Auckland, Melbourne,
Singapore and Toronto

ISBN 1 85732 495 1

Executive Art Editor – Vivienne Brar
Commissioning Editor – Samantha Ward-Dutton
Editors – Claire Musters, Sylvia Sullivan and Tony Stones
Designers – Richard Scott and Nina Pickup
Production Controllers – Liz Carr and Juliette Butler

Produced by Mandarin Offset
Printed in Malaysia

Contents

Key

 Resident

 Summer visitor

 Winter visitor

 Towns and built up areas

 Freshwater (marshes, rivers, lakes)

 Coastal/marine

 Scrub

 Farmland

 Woodland

Introduction

This pocket guide is designed to do three things: to help you identify the birds that use your garden; to give an idea of how they live and interpret what activities they might get up to in your garden; and to provide tips on how to encourage birds to feed and to breed in your garden.

Wherever your garden – be it in the centre of a busy city, on the edge of a wild moor, or on the brink of a cliff – birds are sure to visit it. Of course, not every garden attracts the same species. Some birds are regular visitors to most gardens, but the majority are more selective and will depend on the surrounding habitat. We have chosen species that regularly come to feed on the plants, the invertebrates, or even on the other birds in a garden. It would be impossible to include every bird that has ever appeared in a garden in a pocket guide, but we hope that most readers will find familiar birds here.

The illustrations are designed to help the user identify birds in as many plumages and postures as possible. In particular, we have tried to include flight profiles of most species. Much space has also been given to direct comparisons; not many birds are unmistakable, so comparison and elimination are necessary ingredients to clinching a species' identity. Since this is primarily a book for beginners, we decided to interpose superficially similar birds, such as the pied flycatcher and female chaffinch, as well as the more traditionally perplexing puzzles, such as the willow tit and marsh tit.

No book of this kind would be complete without information on how to encourage more birds into the garden – by feeding them, buying nest-boxes, supplying bird-baths and shelters, and even by planting the kind of vegetation that they like.

Each garden bird has a complex lifestyle, ripe for study by anyone; we hope that this book will inspire people to watch further and discover more about birds.

THE SPECIES PAGES

Each species (apart from the rarer birds on pages 156–159) has a double-page spread, with illustrations and commentary intermixed. The lengths quoted refer to the distance from the tip of the bill to the end of the tail, unless otherwise stated.

The introductory paragraph contains information on the character and garden relevance of the species, and is followed by information on 'Voice' and 'Where Found', except where this information is introduced elsewhere. The geographical range of this guide covers Britain, Ireland and the adjacent parts of northern Europe. Besides location, the 'Where Found' section also gives notes on abundance, and at what time of year the bird may be seen. 'Identification' is usually treated in detail.

What follows is more flexible, but will often include details on 'Feeding', 'Display', 'Nest' and 'Flight'. Also, where they are likely to be seen in gardens, birds in juvenile plumages are described, too, under 'Young', usually after the section on breeding and nesting.

There is a 'Garden Tips' box included for most species. Here, information on how you can help birds in your garden, or hinder less welcome species, is given. Since there is restricted room in this book, we cannot give details of every single food item or nesting site that might benefit the bird, but we can at least offer a guide.

How to encourage birds to visit

Whether your garden is in a city centre or on the edge of a nature reserve, and whether it is a window-box or covers hectares of prime wildlife habitat, you influence how many birds, and what species, use it. Provide food, water, shelter and a place to nest, and birds will show their appreciation just by being there.

FEEDING THE BIRDS DIRECTLY

THE BIRD-TABLE

The bird-table is often just an extension of the kitchen table, where the family's food scraps are put out for birds. A certain inherent variety in the scraps attracts a range of birds – bread for house sparrows, bones for starlings, apples and other fruit for blackbirds. A bird-table doesn't have to be complicated, just a tray set upon a pole or hung from a support. The most important thing is that it's there, and that food is regularly supplied.

Most bird-tables are made of wood. Make sure that the type used is suitable – exterior quality plywood, for example. This will ensure that the bird-table doesn't split and rot. Avoid using wood preservative if you can, as birds prefer a 'natural' surface. Prevent the food from being blown off by putting a rim around the tray. Gaps at the corners make it easier to wipe away uneaten food or other waste, and for rain to drain away. It's a good idea to add a roof to stop both the food and birds getting wet. If you don't have one, drill a few holes in the floor for water to drain away.

A bird-table should be near the cover of a bush or tree, where the birds can flee in case of danger; many species are nervous of visiting open sites. Similarly, if a bird-table is too close to the house, only bolder species, such as pigeons and tits, will use it, at

A standard covered bird-table

least at first. The most successful bird-tables are less than 2–3 m (6½–10 ft) from a tree or bush, and at least 5 m (16½ ft) away from a house. If you want to carry on feeding birds and watching them in winter weather, however, don't put the table too far from the house.

In some gardens, birds regularly fly into windows. Most of these accidents can be avoided by moving feeding stations farther from windows, or by putting up specially-designed window stickers, shaped like birds of prey.

If there are cats in your neighbourhood, every bird-table or other feeder must be positioned even more carefully. The trick is to place the food either out of range of cats, or somewhere where the birds can see them coming. You must prevent cats from being able to conceal themselves within striking range.

You cannot really stop squirrels taking advantage of the food you supply without taking extreme measures. You can, however, make the feeding sites as inaccessible as possible (many 'squirrel-proof' feeders are commercially available), but you'll never really win. Try to enjoy the squirrels for their intelligence and antics.

GROUND STATIONS

Certain species are reluctant to use bird-tables because they are so exposed. Many of these, such as the dunnock and the song thrush, are habitual ground-feeders, so they benefit from food specially put down for them. In rural gardens, grain-eaters such as pheasants, finches and buntings may be attracted to ground stations in winter, and a few lucky farmland locations may have a summer visit from a turtle dove.

Ground stations should be some distance from the bird-table, so that the food provided is not contaminated by droppings from birds above. Food should be placed on a tray or similar, so that it can be removed at night to stop rats taking advantage of it.

Thrushes will visit ground-feeding stations in winter.

HANGING FEEDERS

Tits, and other species that are adapted to feed in trees, often benefit from a more challenging bird-feeder than a bird-table. Blue and great tits, for example, cling upside-down to various types of hanging feeders, and are frequently joined by less common visitors such as nuthatches and siskins.

The excellent range of feeders available allows you to choose which birds you would like to benefit most, and it affords great satisfaction when the purchase has the desired result. More information on feeders can be obtained from a catalogue or more specialized bird-gardening book (see page 2).

You could hang a conventional bird-table from a branch (make sure it is not sturdy enough to support a cat).

This Yankee Droll feeder (left) is specially designed to provide a large amount of seed without excessive spillage, and to keep it dry.

WHAT FOOD TO PUT OUT

The type of food you provide influences the types of birds using the feeding stations. Apart from kitchen scraps, many special bird foods will be appreciated by your visitors and these can be bought commercially. A brief review of foodstuffs for birds follows:

• *Unsalted peanuts* should be provided in every garden, either on the bird-table, or in a hanging feeder. Buy large, high-quality nuts, with a 'Safe Nuts' specification from the Birdfood Standards Association (otherwise they could contain lethal aflatoxins). Tits and finches love peanuts, and they are a sure way to attract siskins, greenfinches, woodpeckers and more unusual species such as long-tailed tits and blackcaps. Ensure that it is difficult for birds to pull a whole peanut from the feeder.

- *Seeds* are popular, and many different mixes can be obtained from stockists. There are many hanging feeders designed especially to dispense them.
- *Fat* provides birds with energy on cold winter days. Provide it on a carcass on the bird-table, or smear it (as suet) into tree bark where a woodpecker or treecreeper will hunt. Alternatively, mix it with seed to form 'bird-cake'.
- *Mealworms* are expensive, but robins love them.
- *Bread* is eaten by many birds. Preferably, it should be brown and soaked in water to prevent it expanding inside birds' stomachs.
- *Fruit* is eaten by thrushes and blackcaps. Store it until late winter or a cold snap, when it will benefit the birds most.
- *Grit* aids digestion, especially for seed-eaters, although it's not actually a food. Sand or gravel will do.

Other good foods are cheese (robins like it), currants, sultanas, baked potatoes (with skins), oatmeal (very popular), pet food, hard-boiled eggs, pastry, stale cake and stale biscuits. This isn't an exhaustive list – experimentation is part of the fun of feeding birds. Avoid salty and dehydrated foods, which can be dangerous.

GENERAL ADVICE ON BIRD FEEDING

Birds are creatures of habit, and it's important that they are fed regularly, especially in freezing weather. The best times are morning and evening, but it doesn't really matter. What does matter is that food comes predictably each day; it's no good feeding the birds for a week and then stopping, to start again at some future date. For their welfare, a little every day is better than a lot every month. If you're going on holiday, make your offerings tail off towards your departure, or ask your neighbours to undertake the feeding.

The question of whether to feed birds in summer has been a controversial one for years. Recently, the trend has been to continue feeding, since garden food can provide a useful supplement for hard-pressed parents. In previous years, it was not recommended as there was evidence that nestlings had been killed by eating the wrong food. However, parent birds know what food suits their nestlings and will try to feed accordingly. The best reason for withholding food in summer is expense, since the birds don't need it.

Finally, birds will benefit from a little hygiene. Try to clean out feeders, especially the bird-table, regularly and move every feeder occasionally, especially if there are piles of droppings beneath.

PROVIDING WATER

Water is as necessary to birds as food, and just as much effort should be put into providing it as conveniently and safely as possible. A bird-bath or a pond, or both, should be an integral part of every birdwatcher's garden.

BIRD-BATHS

Birds will use any water they can find, from elaborate stone baths to puddles. The latter are usually more attractive – architecturally impressive bird-baths usually have sides that are too steep, and water that is too deep. A puddle is perfect because it is shallow, and has different depths of water; birds like to wade into their baths slowly, and don't like to lean too far down when they are drinking.

Water is as necessary to birds as food.

Puddles, of course, are transitory, and a permanent bird-bath should be available. Many suitable types are on the market, with very attractive designs, but an inverted dustbin lid propped up with bricks is just as good. Remember to site the bath carefully, well away from a cat's leap from cover, but near enough to bushes to make birds feel secure. The most successful baths are placed on the ground, in the shade where the water is less likely to evaporate quickly on a hot day.

Remember to clean the bath out regularly as it can quickly become unhygienic. In summer, you will need to top it up every day. In winter, regular supplies of boiling water may be required to prevent it from freezing over. (You could invest in an immersion heater powered from the mains, or a night light placed under the bath.) On no account should you ever add antifreeze or any other chemicals to the water, as these could kill the birds.

PONDS

The great advantage of a pond is that it provides water and a wildlife-rich habitat for the garden. However, it's never enough just to dig a pond and fill it. Suitable oxygenating plants must be provided and bankside vegetation may have to be cut back in the autumn. Fallen leaves must be fished out, and the pond may have to be topped up regularly in hot summer weather. Apart from that, there is little maintenance to worry about.

Although you can buy a garden pond, it's great fun to design and build your own. Good advice on how to do this is given in many wildlife-gardening books. Remember to make sure birds can reach the water – avoid steep sides or put in a ramp for easy access. A small pond will attract birds to bathe and drink; a large pond

Pied wagtails will visit garden ponds.

will attract water birds. Several of the birds in this book, such as kingfishers and grey wagtails, will only use large garden ponds.

Many people complain about their fish being taken by herons, or tadpoles being taken by birds such as crows and blackbirds. If fish are to be protected, the only real safeguard is netting. But the fact is, animals eat each other. Sparrowhawks might treat your bird-table like a fast-food restaurant, but it is an impressive sight when they whisk away a blue tit with a flick of the wings and talons. Faced with such dilemmas, it's best to be philosophical.

BIRD GARDENING

No amount of food provision will affect your garden as a habitat for birds; to create good surroundings, you must plant the right kinds of trees, shrubs and flowers.

By and large, the best plants to grow are those that are native to this country. This makes sense, because bird and plant have had plenty of time over the centuries to adapt to one another. And, more importantly, each native plant comes with its own associated invertebrates. It goes without saying that pesticides are not compatible with wildlife gardening except in extreme circumstances.

Holly is an ideal berry-bearing tree to plant – the prickly leaves act as a barrier to cats.

TREES
You can almost place an order for a bird species when you plant a tree, although it may take some time for it to arrive! After 20 years of growth, for example, birches might attract redpolls. If possible, a garden should have a hedge and tall, reasonably spaced standard trees. If there's a choice, the hedge is the more important, but the strength of the garden habitat is in its variety.

A few trees to consider: hawthorn is a wonderful hedge tree, with lots of cover all year round and highly-rated berries in the autumn – a must; holly is much the same, and its prickly leaves can also form a deterrent for cats (plant female hollies if you want berries); rowan is another good berry tree for those who dream of waxwings, supplying many other birds while you wait – and it doesn't outgrow the garden; alder attracts siskins, goldfinches and even willow tits, and grows fast; goat (pussy) willow grows speedily and vigorously and provides early spring flowers; birch attracts many species, is fast-growing and very beautiful. Don't neglect fruit trees such as apples and cherries, but select wild strains.

Decide early on whether you or the birds will get the fruit, or there will be war. Plant classical British trees such as oak, beech or ash in large gardens – these will prove a great bonus in years to come.

For those who like a variety of birds, conifers certainly have a place, but they should never dominate a garden. Goldcrests and coal tits prefer them for breeding, and crossbills need them at all times. The Scots pine or the yew are the best natives. Cypress, an 'exotic', has very thick foliage, which is ideal for roosting birds (especially finches) in the winter, and for nesting blackbirds and song thrushes in the spring.

SHRUBS AND CLIMBERS

Plant native shrubs as a priority. Willows, spindle, guelder rose and hazel are good examples, and elder attracts more species of birds to its berries than any other. One exception to the 'natives-only' rule is buddleia, or 'butterfly bush', which has a magnetic draw for butterflies and other insects. Other popular garden shrubs that are good for birds are cotoneaster, pyracantha and berberis, which provide berries or nesting sites. One shrub to be avoided is rhododendron, which is as useless a bird plant as it is beautiful. It's invasive, and has degraded large areas of formerly good woodland throughout Britain. Leave it at the garden centre.

The much-maligned bramble is good for the garden if controlled; it provides cover, protection, lots of insects and berries.

CLIMBERS

These are a must. Ivy is a wonderful garden plant, offering cover, berries and flowers. The flowers come out late in the year, prolonging the insect season for many birds. Honeysuckle, also a native, has a lovely smell and is great for insects, especially moths.

FLOWERS

Almost any flower that attracts insects, or provides seeds, will be appreciated by birds. A few recommended plants: poppy, scabious, sweet william, Michaelmas daisy, sunflower (for greenfinches), thistles (for goldfinches), lavender, snapdragon, corncockle, *Sedum spectabile*, rosemary, thyme, red-hot pokers, *Daphne mezereum*, teasel.

Buddleia is known as the butterfly bush. Here, a spotted flycatcher takes advantage of the food supply.

GRASSES AND LAWNS

Every bird garden should have a lawn. Apart from providing good conditions for ground-feeding birds like blackbirds, starlings and robins, a lawn will also make them easier to watch, and provide an extra site where food can be laid down. If you have a large area of lawn, consider turning some of it into a wildflower meadow, which will increase the wildlife richness of the garden.

Providing a place to nest

The measure of a good bird garden is probably not how many birds feed in it, but how many breed in it. Suburban areas are so full of nooks and crannies that they allow for a high density of breeding birds, so a little extra encouragement goes a long way.

NEST-SITES

In assessing the suitability of your garden, alert yourself to possible nest-sites – perhaps an old tree could be left to rot, the old shed could be left open, a small hole could be made in the eaves, the bramble could be allowed to grow on the edge of the border. An exercise like this may make your garden better for birds with a minimum of cost in time and effort. One thing will soon become apparent: if your garden is tidy and rigorously managed, the options for birds will be restricted.

Hedges should be trimmed to maintain their thickness; the lawn must be mown regularly (a wild area of grass is very unlikely to attract nesting birds); wild areas, especially of creepers or weeds, should be kept or promoted; trees should be allowed to age and rot where safety permits; neglected parts of buildings should be spared all but essential maintenance; piles of clippings or logs should be left; and the compost heap should be just that – a heap. There are many things you can do to select nests for birds before they do.

NEST-BOXES

Nest-boxes are especially rewarding because they make it very easy to follow birds' progress step-by-step.Good advice on how to make nest-boxes is available in various bird-gardening books, or you can get them from, for example, the RSPB (see page 2). Garden

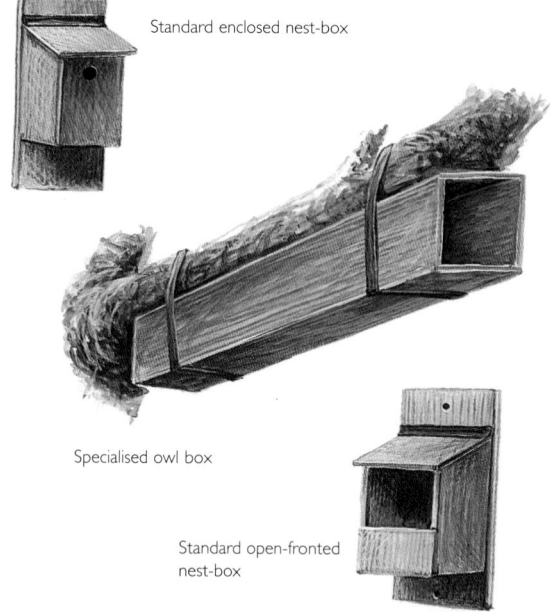

Standard enclosed nest-box

Specialised owl box

Standard open-fronted nest-box

centres are not ideal places to buy nest-boxes or obtain advice. For example, avoid the bird-table-cum-nest-box – birds are very territorial, and the unfortunate occupants will suffer great stress from the presence of feeding birds close to their nest. Any nest-box with a perch by the hole might make access easier for a predator. It is best to get the box from a specialist supplier.

There are a great many types of nest-box, because the requirements of each species are different. A coal tit, for example, needs a smaller entrance hole than a great tit, simply to keep the latter from evicting it when competition arises. And competition does arise, constantly: starlings fight with sparrows, which fight with tits, which fight with pied flycatchers, which fight with nuthatches, only to be supplanted by ring-necked parakeets. Some birds can be encouraged by a box with an open front – robins, pied wagtails and even redstarts are examples. Others may be persuaded to nest in nests tailor-made for them: there are treecreeper-boxes, kestrel-boxes, tawny owl-boxes, and house martin-boxes.

There are a few ground rules to follow. First, don't put up too many in too small a space – birds are territorial around their nest-sites, and need space around them. One or two boxes in the average garden is enough. Secondly, introduce a nest-box before the breeding season begins, preferably in the autumn; the box will weather satisfactorily before summer comes, and may provide winter roosting. Thirdly, clean out a used nest-box at the end of the season, in October or November, to kill any parasites that might be around. Wash in boiling water, not using any kind of insecticide.

The siting of a nest-box is extremely important. It must be out of range of disturbance – about 2 m (6½ ft) up a tree trunk or wall could be a sensible place, ie, not placed in a rain channel, not south-facing (too much sun can overheat eggs or chicks), and facing away from prevailing winds and rain. Open-fronted nest-boxes are particularly vulnerable and should be placed in thick cover. However much trouble you take, it might be several seasons before a box is deemed suitable by the birds.

One final piece of advice: don't make regular checks on the progress of your tenants. Leave them alone throughout the season, and be happy to watch everything from the outside. Too much interference could lead to disaster.

NEST PREDATORS

One of the worst experiences for a garden birdwatcher is to watch young birds being attacked by a predator. The sight of a cat playing with a fledgling, or a magpie robbing a nest, can be upsetting. So, what can be done? Sadly, there is little you can do. Fledglings must learn to survive; only the 'fittest' in every sense will do so.

You can't stop a cat hunting birds. If it's your own cat, you could fix a bell to its collar to alert birds, but if it's a neighbour's, you'll have to deter it some other way. You could grow cat-proof hedges of holly and other prickly plants, but the only real deterrent, is to hire a full-time cat-chaser to keep them away – a dog.

Grey squirrels are a menace to nesting birds, taking eggs and young. Do everything you can to discourage them.

Magpies have become a serious problem in recent times. Although they don't really affect the populations of smaller species, blackbirds, song thrushes and chaffinches (species that build open-cup nests) do suffer. Once again, there isn't much you can do.

In some areas, great-spotted woodpeckers will hack their way through the side of a nest-box, especially near the hole, to take away young birds – this is a serious problem in some areas. Many nest-boxes come with a metal plate to protect the occupants from this rather exotic form of nest predation.

Finally, should you find a helpless nestling or fledgling on your lawn – leave it alone. If it's a nestling (a baby bird appearing naked, tiny and helpless), it will probably die whatever you do; if it's a fledgling (a young bird appearing well-feathered but unkempt), it's probably waiting for you to leave so that its parents can feed it. Whatever good motives you have, please don't intervene.

There is little you can do to stop a cat hunting birds. If you own a cat, attach a bell to its collar.

PROVIDING SHELTER

Shelter is important to birds at all times, but especially in winter. When birds sleep, they need places that are relatively warm, dry and free from wind. Grow a few thick bushes in the garden, or a hedge, or both. Keep nest-boxes outside all winter, since they are ideal as roost-sites for small birds – up to 60 wrens have been found in a single box. Also, leave a small crack in your garden shed, garage or even the roof, where birds might be able to get in.

Identifying the birds in your garden

If you are a beginner to birdwatching, a good starting point would be to flick through the pages of this book when you have time. The images will begin to stick in your mind and you'll develop a knowledge of the range of shapes and colours. If you wish to progress further, there comes a point when bills, rumps, wing-bars and bibs, crown-stripes and coverts must enter the equation.

SIZE The first feature to check is size. 'Brown, with a short tail' could refer to a wren and it could refer to a female ostrich. No description is complete without an estimate of size, preferably with reference to a similar species whose dimensions are known. Of the two common, greenish finches that use hanging feeders, one is sparrow-sized (greenfinch), and one is blue tit-sized (siskin). Size is easily distorted by viewing conditions – birds look larger when they are back-lit or silhouetted.

SHAPE Next, check the shape. Some birds have distinctive shapes, but most are distinguishable by subtleties in the shapes of bill, wings, head or tail. The bill shape is a clue to the bird's eating habits, and, most especially, distinguishes seed-eaters (thick bills) from insect-eaters (thin bills). The shape of the wings is useful for distinguishing swifts, swallows and house martins, for example; head shape is useful for whitethroats and skylarks, rooks and crows; and tail shape is good for blue tits and siskins, rooks and crows, and the wagtails. Each of these is one example among many.

COLOUR Not much need be said about this, except that overall colour is less useful than the colour of certain parts of the body. Many birds have specially coloured rumps; it's as if they were all designed with birdwatchers in mind. Chaffinches have green rumps, bramblings and bullfinches have white rumps, and serins have yellow rumps, for example. When these are put together with colourful wing-bars and head patterns, the identification of finches, and many other birds, becomes straightforward. Useful spots, stripes and patches of colour, useful for identification, are known as 'field marks'.

BEHAVIOUR Behaviour is an important clue to identification. Strictly speaking, every single bird in the world has slightly different behaviour. Yet the most useful aspects of behaviour are those it will engage in while being watched: a wagtail wags its tail, a swallow swoops low over a field, a treecreeper shuffles up a tree trunk, a wren cocks its tail. The combination of a species' shape,

The treecreeper (above) always creeps up trees. The nuthatch (right) can creep up or down.

movements and demeanour, its 'character', is known as 'jizz'. If you do a lot of birdwatching, you'll find yourself identifying birds by jizz almost at a glance.

SONGS AND CALLS It's a good idea to get to know the various songs and calls, because some species do make very distinctive sounds and the voices of others can be learned quite easily with a little practice. The best way to learn a song is to listen to one, and then to locate and identify the singer by sight. There are many cassettes and CDs available which will help you to learn the songs and calls. There's no doubt that the world of bird sounds opens up many new horizons for every birdwatcher; you'll find more birds, and identification becomes much easier.

TOPOGRAPHY

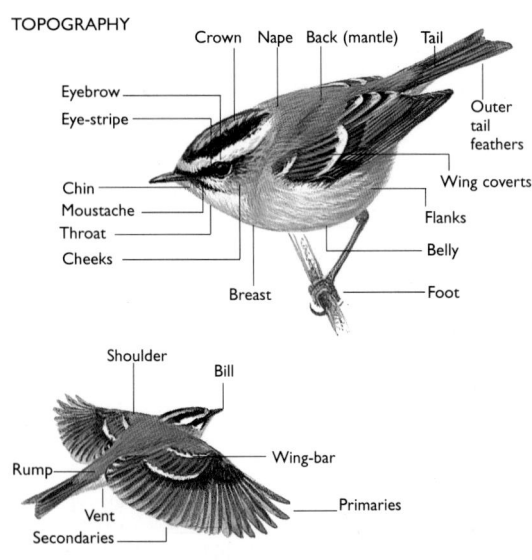

HABITAT, RANGE AND TIME OF YEAR These three indirect clues to identification are essential. All the birds in this book occur in gardens, of course, but in reality most are visitors from another habitat (for example, woodland). What habitat lies around your garden? Are you in the geographical range the bird is supposed to inhabit? If not, your identification may need checking. Many birds have particular seasons when they are present in the garden: siskins in winter, swallows in summer, for example. Although birds do break the rules, the season of the year is a very good clue when you are narrowing down a set of possibilities.

EQUIPMENT FOR BIRDWATCHING

Although you need only a book and a bird-table at the start of your hobby, a notebook (to keep a record of your visitors) and a pair of binoculars will help later on. Buy binoculars from a specialist seller who understands the needs of birdwatchers; avoid the high-street stores. All binoculars have a specification signified by two figures, for example, 8 x 30. The first figure is the magnification, the second is the diameter of the objective (larger) lens in millimetres. The latter gives an idea of how much light enters the binoculars. A magnification of between 7 and 10 is enough. For garden bird-watching, a decent pair of 8 x 40s should suffice, and will cost in the region of £120.

Glossary

Breeding season: Time of year when bird is involved in reproductive behaviour. Usually covers egg-laying to feeding young out of the nest.

Call: Sound made by any bird, in response to a given situation such as alarm. Also for keeping flocks together. Usually brief.

Faecal sac: Aggregation of faeces from a nestling, carried away from the nest by a parent.

First-winter: A bird in its first winter of life (hatched previous summer). Also refers to plumage adopted by such birds (lasts until the following spring).

First-year: A bird living its first year of life, and plumage thereof.

Fledgling: Young bird that has feathers and has left the nest.

Flight feathers: Feathers of the wing and tail.

Foraging: The process of looking for food, as opposed to eating.

Immature: Any plumage adopted before adult. Usually refers to a bird which takes one or more years to mature (eg, a gull).

Introduced: A species which came to this country only because of human actions, deliberate or otherwise. Opposite of native.

Juvenile: Young birds that have left the nest, and are no longer dependent on parents. Also refers to that plumage.

Local: Only found in a few scattered places.

Migration: Movement from one place to another of a significant proportion of the population. Mostly in spring and autumn.

Nestling: Unfeathered chick confined to nest, dependent on parents.

Raptor: A day-flying bird of prey.

Resident: Species present all year, although individuals may move.

Song: Usually complex signal given by a male bird to state territorial ownership or to attract a mate. Almost always has some reproductive significance.

Undulating flight: Flight which rises and falls rhythmically, as wing-beats start and stop.

Grey heron *Ardea cinerea*

There's no mistaking the tall, statuesque, stately heron, by far the largest bird to visit most gardens. Often seen standing over a pond, it is a fish-eater which hunts by stealth and surprise. Its long legs allow it to wade deep into water, which it does with an almost mechanical smoothness, and its long neck can be stretched out at lightning speed to grab unsuspecting prey. Such a hunting method relies on stillness and patience, just as it does for every fisherman! Apart from fish, it also eats amphibians and waterside mammals, and occasionally birds such as ducklings find a place on the menu. The heron is wary, quick to fly off at the slightest disturbance; when visiting garden ponds, it prefers to come early in the morning. Ponds in small, enclosed gardens with high walls are usually shunned as they are too risky to visit.

FISHING
A heron stands motion-less over a garden pond, waiting for a fish. Usually seen singly, each heron has its own year-round territory. Prey under control is sometimes stabbed to death.

Adult has black crown-stripe and plume

Black shoulder

Dagger-like bill for grabbing fish

No black crown-stripe

YOUNG
More uniformly grey in colour

YOUNG
Young birds are greyer, and lack black crown-stripe. Learning to catch fish is difficult, and youngsters often make mistakes: this one has selected a pond with sides that are too steep.

VOICE
Loud, very irritable 'fraank!', given mostly in flight.

WHERE FOUND
Common throughout the area wherever there is fresh water. Resident.

FLIGHT

The wings are arched and beaten slowly and heavily, with the long legs trailing behind. The neck is retracted and bulging. Herons are often harassed by crows and other birds because in flight they resemble large birds of prey.

Wings arched

Legs trailing

Bill turns bright pink in early breeding season

PLUMAGE CARE

Sunbathing birds adopt this ecstatic posture. Special feathers on the belly make powder, and a gland on the rump produces preen-oil (like most birds). One claw on the foot is toothed, and 'combs' powder and oil through plumage to remove fish oil and other detritus.

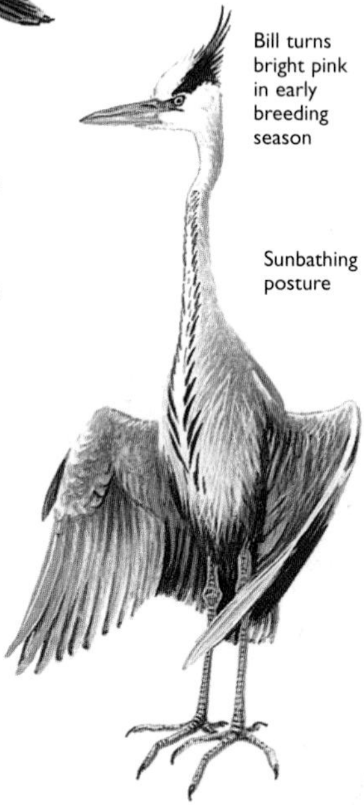

Sunbathing posture

Hunched posture common

BREEDING

Grey herons nest colonially, high in trees, building huge stick structures. Building or refurbishment begins very early in the season, often late January. This may be to allow the young time to learn to fish, before hard times follow during winter.

GARDEN TIPS

Herons may visit ponds, especially in more spacious gardens. They usually visit in the early morning and individuals will soon become regular visitors if there are plenty of fish to catch. If there's a conflict of interest, try putting a trip-wire around the edge of the pond or netting over the water, which makes it more difficult for the birds to fish. Birds avoid 'territory-holding' plastic herons, too, but these can look a little incongruous in a small garden.

19

Mallard *Anas platyrhynchos*

Every conceivable patch of water seems to attract this duck, whether it be a park lake, a river or a transient puddle. It's the only wild duck species at all likely to be seen in gardens, and it will take advantage of even moderately-sized ponds. It's a member of a group of species known as 'dabbling' ducks, which obtain their food from the surface of the water or by up-ending, but not by diving (the ducklings do dive, however). Although primarily aquatic, mallards don't necessarily nest close to water, so watch out for broods spilling from unexpected places such as tree-holes or thick flowerbeds. Ducklings commonly hold up traffic while crossing roads on their way to water. Like all ducks, mallards look ungainly on land, but are at ease on water and in flight.

VOICE
The familiar quacking. Only the females give the series of quacks sounding like a 'belly-laugh'.

WHERE FOUND
Abundant wherever there is water.

MALE

Green head

Ash-brown body

FLIGHT
Mallards 'spring' from the water surface when disturbed. Flight agile and fast (ducks are among the fastest flying birds).

FEMALE

Duller brown

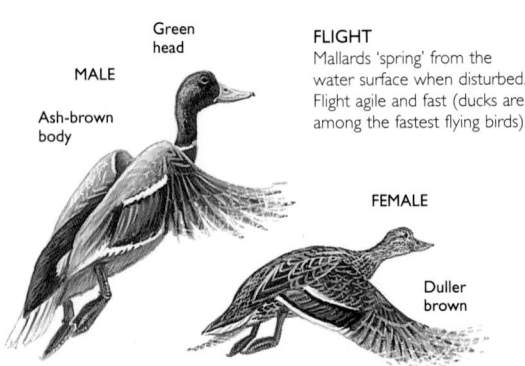

PLUMAGE
Males and females look quite different. The male has an iridescent green head, ash-brown body, curled-up tail. Bill colours vary. Colourful bar on secondaries (the speculum) is same on both sexes – purplish, bordered with white. Each species of duck has a different speculum pattern.

BREEDING

Ten or more eggs are laid and ducklings leave the
nest before they are a day old. The colourful
drake is not involved in incubation or
chick-rearing.

Male in drab
'eclipse' plumage

ECLIPSE PLUMAGE

In mid-summer, males
move away to moult
(females follow later).
They lose their wing
feathers all at once and
become temporarily
flightless, at the same
time assuming a drab
body plumage similar
to that of the female.
This so-called 'eclipse'
plumage gives them
protective camouflage
until they can fly again a
few weeks later.

Displaying
males

DISPLAY

In winter and spring, watch for the subtle displays of mallards. This
stretching and mock-preening is accompanied by quiet whistles. The
'water-flick' is intentional.

Buzzard *Buteo buteo*

Dwarfing the crows that often mob it, the impressive buzzard is the largest common bird of prey in Britain. It is most often seen in flight, soaring and circling high over fields or woodland. In the west and north of Britain, where it is common, it is also regularly seen over gardens. Individual buzzards are highly territorial, mounting regular soaring patrols on their boundaries; neighbours doing this often share the same thermals. Buzzards take a variety of live prey, using three different hunting techniques: pouncing on small mammals, such as voles or rabbits, from soaring or hovering flight; pouncing on mammals or birds from a perched position; and walking on the ground, foraging for insects and worms.

VOICE
Marvellously evocative, wild mewing 'whee-ew', with emphasis on the first syllable. Very distinctive.

WHERE FOUND
Widespread resident in the west and north, rare in central and south-east England.

When soaring or circling, the wings are held in a shallow 'V'

Minor aerial scuffles do break out in territorial rivalry

Pale patch at base of primaries

Broad wings

Collecting nest material

Short tail

Prominent 'fingers'

IDENTIFICATION
Predominantly dark brown, but some are redder. In fact, every bird has slightly different plumage. Look for the large size, very broad wings with prominent 'fingers' at the end, and distinctly short tail, often fanned.

Wingspan
113–128 cm
(45–51 in)

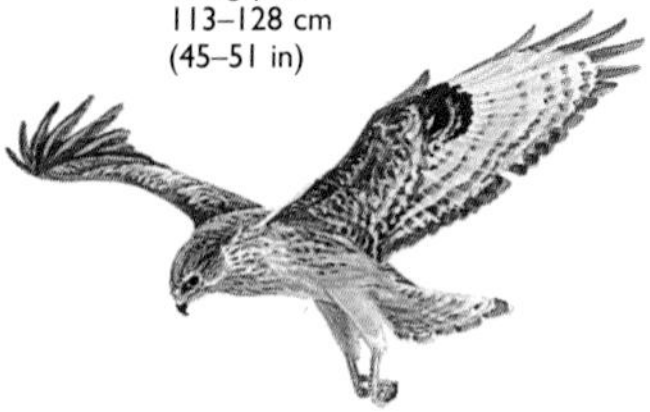

HUNTING
Usually buzzards hang in the wind, rather than hover. Some buzzards practise this more than others.

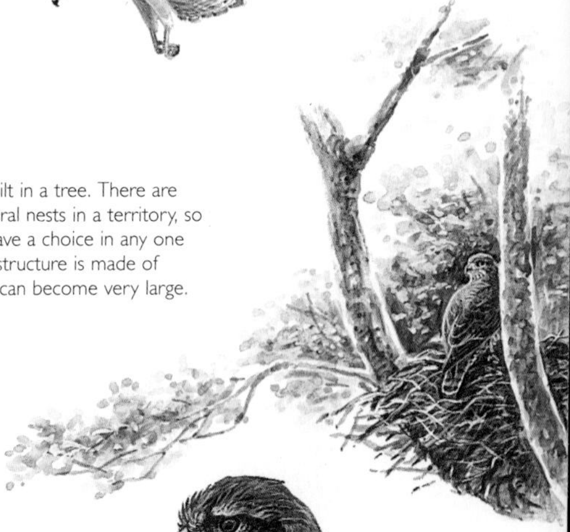

NEST
Usually built in a tree. There are often several nests in a territory, so the pair have a choice in any one year. The structure is made of sticks and can become very large.

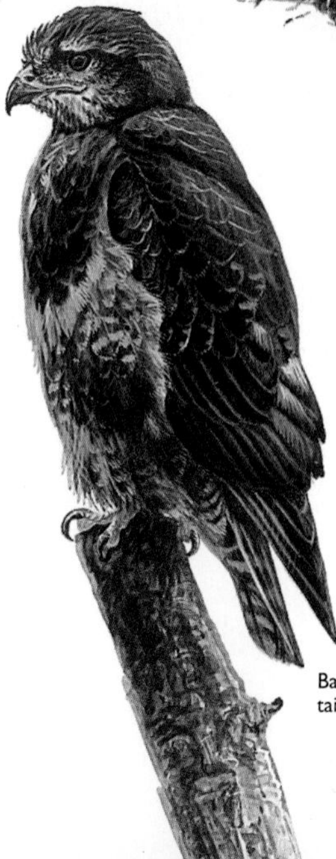

Pale breast-band

PERCHING
A bird sits patiently on a low post, where it can look down periodically for prey. Buzzards often use this hunting method in bad weather, when flying is difficult. When perched, this species presents a bulky frame, the round head and heavy chest lending the bird a rather 'macho' appearance. There is often a pale band across the breast.

Barred
tail

23

Sparrowhawk *Accipiter nisus*

Shattering the peace of the bird-feeding station by its lightning aerial strikes, the sparrowhawk provides the most brutal drama of the garden arena. Using the element of surprise, it hunts small birds, sometimes snatching them from bird-tables in front of astonished onlookers. But usually all we see is a dashing shape disappearing over a fence or rooftop, or into thick foliage. By then there has been a kill, or a narrow escape! The sparrowhawk is well-adapted for a life of hunting: its sight is superb, enabling it to pick out small birds from several hundred metres; the wings and tail enable it to twist and turn acrobatically and build up speed fast; and the talons and bill are sharp and lethal.

WHERE FOUND
Widespread, locally common resident. A regular sight in suburban gardens. Mostly a woodland bird.

HUNTING
Most victims are caught in flight, by the talons, but a minority are chased when they land and are trapped on the ground.

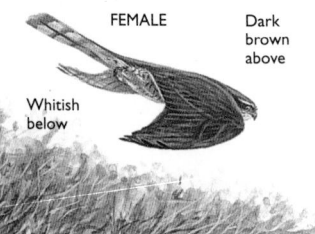

FEMALE

Dark brown above

Whitish below

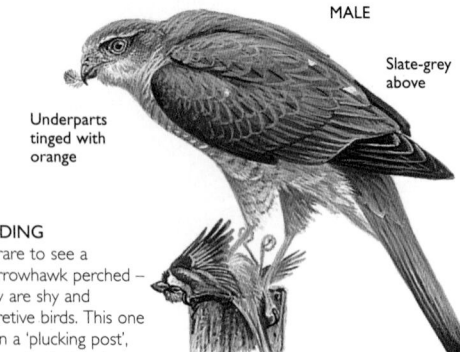

MALE

Slate-grey above

Underparts tinged with orange

FEEDING
It's rare to see a sparrowhawk perched – they are shy and secretive birds. This one is on a 'plucking post', devouring its latest capture. One or two meals a day will suffice in winter, but up to 10 are required to feed a growing brood in summer months.

VOICE
Ringing call rarely heard, but the presence of a sparrowhawk overhead will elicit sharp, high-pitched 'seee' calls from other birds.

SIZE OF SEXES

Male is much smaller than female. Outside the breeding season, the two birds follow different diets to avoid competition between them: the male takes smaller birds (tits, finches), the female larger birds (thrushes, starlings).

NEST

Built in a tall tree, usually a conifer, often right up against the trunk. Here a male sparrowhawk brings food to the nest.

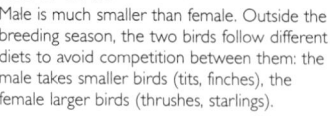

FLIGHT

Diagnostic flap- flap- glide flight sequence. Sparrowhawks never hover (compare kestrel, next page). Birds soar in fine weather, especially in springtime.

Wingspan 55–70 cm (22–28 in)

Broad, blunt wings

Closed, square-ended tail

DISPLAY

In courtship display, birds alternately drop down and fly upwards in a steep curve, describing a gigantic 'U'. The performance ends with a spectacular dive from a great height.

GARDEN TIPS

Sparrowhawks will readily take small birds from feeders. You can discourage them from doing this by placing food for small birds under the cover of thick branches (make sure that this is inaccessible to cats). But really, you are priviledged if they hunt in your garden.

Kestrel *Falco tinnunculus*

The kestrel is the bird of prey most often seen by people – over motorways, over farmland, and even right in the hearts of cities. In urban settings, tall buildings are popular nest-sites, and here the birds' activities can offer welcome distraction for office workers and for those who live many floors up. Kestrels occur in suburban gardens, too. Although predatory, they are less likely to attack birds at feeding stations than sparrowhawks, relying instead on a wider diet of small mammals, insects and earthworms, as well as birds. Although kestrels and sparrowhawks are similar in shape and size, the sparrowhawk never hovers, and kestrels hover frequently. They also have several other hunting methods, including pouncing on prey from a perched position, and foraging on the ground. Kestrels have exceptional sight, and occasionally hunt by moonlight.

VOICE
At the nest-site it utters a hoarse, unmusical laugh; this intensifies and becomes quavering and broken during display.

WHERE FOUND
Very common and widespread resident. Open country and waste ground.

MALE

Slate-grey head

FEMALE
Red/brown head and tail

Dark rust-coloured back

Smaller than female

Slate-grey tail

Tail has more bars

PAIR AT THE NEST
The male has brought in a mouse. As in most birds of prey, the male does all the hunting for his family until the young are quite well-grown.

YOUNG

YOUNG
Resemble the female, but less fierce-looking. In all plumages, bars go down the breast. In sparrowhawk, go across breast.

Vertical streaks on breast

26

HOVERING

If it hovers, it must be a kestrel – the diagnostic hunting method of this small raptor. The bird holds its head still, even though the wings, body and tail move. When prey is sighted, a bird usually 'homes in' on its meal before the final dive and strike.

Wingspan 71–80 cm (28–32 in)

Rounded tail spread when hovering

Homing in

Pointed wings

Final strike

KESTREL

Black tail band

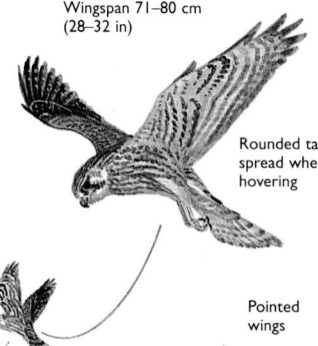

PLUMAGE

Male kestrel has one thick bar at end of tail, very chestnut back. Black primaries on both sexes. Wings long, distinctly pointed. Male sparrowhawk slate blue-grey above, female brown. Primaries not black. Sparrowhawk underside orange in male. Compare the soaring sparrowhawk: it's a thicker bird, with much broader and blunter wings.

SPARROWHAWK

Broader, blunter wings

FLIGHT

When flying level, the kestrel has a rather 'flappy' flight, with rapid wing-beats.

GARDEN TIPS

Kestrels may take scraps from bird-tables. They often attack starlings, their favourite bird food. Kestrels use open-fronted 'kestrel-boxes' put in trees or on tall buildings.

27

Pheasant *Phasianus colchicus*

Exotic in shape and colour, the pheasant is a familiar bird of open fields, farmland and light patches of woodland. The male is unmistakable: an extravagant mixture of coppery red, green and brown plumage, and with a spectacularly long tail. The female is smaller, cryptically coloured with pale buff plumage and a shorter tail. This is a terrestrial species, living most of its life on the ground, foraging for both animal and vegetable food unearthed by scratching among earth and litter. Many thousands of pheasants are released annually by gamekeepers for shooting; they are good sport and excellent eating. Understandably shy, some pheasants can be coaxed into larger gardens and encouraged to visit feeding stations on the ground. Sometimes bushy trees in gardens are also used for roosting at night; the birds come together in small groups and rest on the branches, making their irritable coughing calls as they sort out who sits where.

HAREM

This male accompanies several females, taking grain put out for chickens. Polygyny (one male, several females) is the norm, with occasionally up to 12 in one harem. The partners' relationship will be slight; all nesting duties are performed by the female.

FEMALE

MALE

WHERE FOUND

Common and widespread resident. Farmland, roadsides.

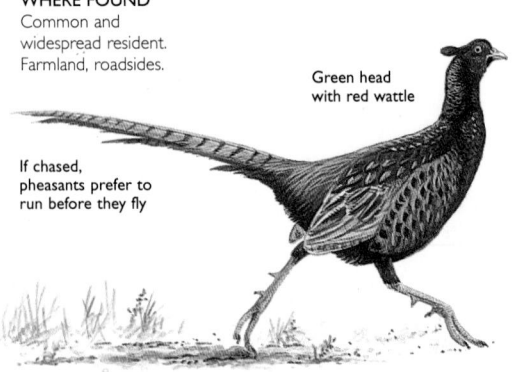

Green head with red wattle

If chased, pheasants prefer to run before they fly

PLUMAGE

Details of the colourful plumage vary between individual males, but most have a red wattle, green head and at least some coppery coloration.

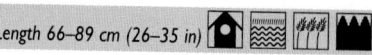
FIGHTS AND DISPLAYS

In spring, vicious territorial encounters between rival males occur. The feet are armed with spurs, which can cause serious injury.

To proclaim its territory, a male 'coughs' and flaps its wings. This green form of male is uncommon

NEST

The female's camouflaged plumage is perfect for the leaf-litter. Clutches are large – 11 is average – and losses are high even though she accompanies her brood, sometimes with the male present too, from the moment they hatch.

JUVENILE

Clattering flight

FLIGHT

When disturbed, birds burst away with a clatter of wings and an explosion of coughing calls. When flying level, the birds stay low, the wings are beaten rapidly and there are periodic glides.

Moorhen *Gallinula chloropus*

Present wherever there is vegetation-fringed fresh water, the moorhen is a regular visitor to gardens with large ponds or streams. It has a nervous disposition, walking deliberately with constant jittery flicks of the tail, but soon becomes tame where supplied with various kinds of scraps. It even flies up to bird-tables at times, although its proper food consists of vegetation and some aquatic insects. On the water it swims with a laboured bobbing of its head back and forth. When approached threateningly on land, it will run head-down, wings flapping, half-flying into the nearest cover. Its use of land and water makes it a truly amphibious bird.

IDENTIFICATION
Adult distinctive. Dark, slaty plumage relieved by white line along midriff. Beak red with a yellow tip. Legs long and green with elongated, unwebbed toes. Saucy red garters above the knees! Long, green toes are perfect for clambering around in clumps of iris, reeds and long grass, and for climbing in trees.

VOICE
A variety of clucks and gurgles. Most distinctive sound is a sharp, bubbly 'kurruk!'

ADULT

Red beak with yellow tip

Dark, slaty plumage

Long, green legs with red 'garter' above knee

WHERE FOUND
Common and widespread resident. Any fresh water with some vegetation.

SIMILAR SPECIES
The coot is a close relative of the moorhen, which prefers large areas of open water. Coots have blue, lobed feet and dive constantly. Moorhens don't dive.

Tail flicked

MOORHEN

Red- and orange bill

COOT

White mid-line and undertail

All black

White frontal shield

COMBAT

In spring, birds become aggressively territorial, with fights and skirmishes breaking out everywhere. Aggressively inclined birds display, putting their heads down and their tails up, the latter so that the white undertail is shown to advantage. But if posturing, noise and chasing do not solve the dispute, the birds take to the water and fight with their feet.

NEST

Moorhens build lots of nests, constructing cups of grass and leaves on or just above the water level.

Sometimes more than one female lays in the same nest. This 'egg-dumping' habit is quite common, and means a female moorhen is more productive than if she just looked after her own hatchlings.

YOUNG

Brown plumage

CHICK

Fluffy black ball with legs

Dull bill

YOUNG

Youngsters sometimes help their parents with looking after a later brood in the same summer they themselves hatched – this is very unusual among birds.

Black-headed gull *Larus ridibundus*

Most gulls seen inland in winter will be of this species. It's the gull that forages over arable land, playing fields, lakes and ponds, and is also the most commonest visitor to gardens. Large areas of grass offer worms and other invertebrates, but in gardens it will come for scraps, bread, fat, carcasses – in fact, almost anything. All gulls prefer open situations, so they will avoid visiting bird-tables near cover. Bands of them commonly perch on rooftops, especially near popular feeding areas, and small groups patrol the neighbourhood, searching for easy food. In some areas, they have learned to catch food thrown to them, squabbling over any items dropped. Gull identification is difficult, due to a confusing series of plumages as individuals mature, but look for colour of the bill and legs.

ADULT PLUMAGE – SUMMER AND WINTER

In winter: distinctive dark smudge behind eye. Summer plumage (developed in some individuals from February onwards); smudge grows into chocolate-brow (not black) hood.

WINTER

VOICE

A distinctive harsh, rolling call or series of calls, grating, unlike all other gulls.

Dark smudge behind eye

SUMMER

Chocolate-brown hood

MIXED FLOCK

Black-headed gull is the smallest common species of gull, and the only one with red bill and red legs in adult plumage. Common gull is slightly larger with yellow-green or grey legs, a yellow bill and a darker back with white spots ('mirrors') on primaries.

First winter

Adult summer

Common gull

Adult winter

WHERE FOUND
Widespread and very common. More local, and more coastal, in the breeding season.

YOUNG
Young birds have brown markings on wings, a black band across the tail, an orange-brown bill (with black tip), and, sometimes, orange legs.

Black tail band

FIRST WINTER

FIRST WINTER
'First winters' are youngsters in their first winter of life, having hatched the previous summer.

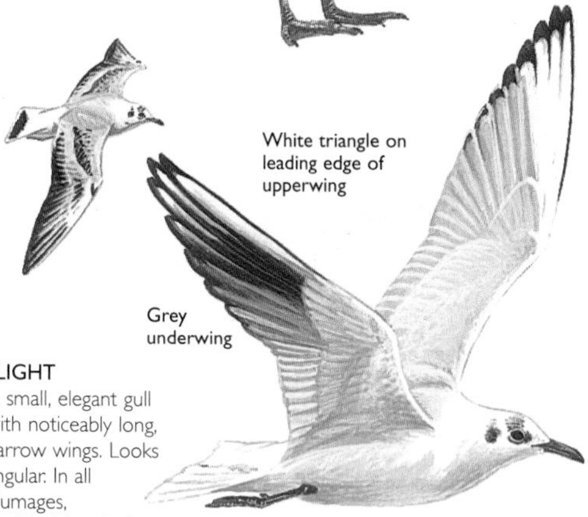

Brown markings on wings

Orange legs

White triangle on leading edge of upperwing

Grey underwing

FLIGHT
A small, elegant gull with noticeably long, narrow wings. Looks angular. In all plumages, the black-headed gull can be distinguished by a white triangle on leading edge of upperwing, seen on no other widespread species. Underwing is grey, with white streak along tip bordered by dark feathering.

ROOSTING FLOCKS
In regions with reservoirs, vast lines of gulls can be seen flying over, commuting to roost on these waters. Flocks often assume 'V'-formation, or spiralling swirls.

Common gull *Larus canus (including herring gull)*

An easily overlooked species, which doesn't really deserve the name 'common' gull, since it is greatly outnumbered by black-headed and herring gulls wherever it occurs (the former inland, the latter on the coast). Even so, the common gull is still quite numerous, especially in winter. It's most often seen among black-headed gull flocks, joining them on fields, on rooftops and flying over gardens. Like the black-headed gull, it sometimes combs lawns for invertebrates, and more occasionally takes scraps from bird-tables.

WHERE FOUND
Widespread and fairly common in winter, on playing fields, agricultural land, etc. Breeds in Scotland, quite widespread.

WINTER PLUMAGE
Has yellowish or grey legs and bill, and dark flecks (but not black-headed gull's smudge) on head.

Dark flecks on head

WINTER COMMON GULL

Smaller than herring gull

SUMMER PLUMAGE
Loses flecks on the head. Yellower legs. In all plumages shows dark eye and gentle expression.

ADULT
Size is close to black-headed gull, plumage is close to herring gull.

No flecks on head

SUMMER COMMON GULL

Gentle facial expression

VOICE
A distinctive, cat-like wailing call, higher-pitched than other gulls, and sometimes ear-splitting.

Dark eye

FLIGHT
Compare to herring gull (opposite). Wing pattern similar, but white spots ('mirrors') on black wing-tips are larger.

FIRST WINTER

Large white spots ('mirrors') on black wing-tips

SIMILAR SPECIES

The larger herring gull is abundant all round our coasts, where its various calls – wailing, whinnying and muttering – are commonly heard. In contrast, it is rather uncommon inland. Where they patronise seaside gardens, herring gulls often steal from bird-tables and generally cause commotion wherever they go. They commonly nest on rooftops, a recently acquired habit which is a mixed blessing to householders. Being omnivores, these gulls take advantage of scraps of all sorts, but they particularly love fish, not just herrings and will gather in flocks to scavenge outside seaside fast-food shops. There is a great variety of plumages; youngsters take four years to mature, changing their plumage between summer and winter. Adults are basically grey, while the youngsters are basically brown.

ADULT HERRING GULL

Large, as big as a large duck. Pink legs at all times. Yellow bill has blood-red spot.

Dark flecks on head

Pale eye

Yellow bill with blood-red spot

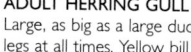
ADULT WINTER HERRING GULL

Large size

HERRING GULL PLUMAGES

In winter, adults have dark flecks on the head, like the common gull, but are always distinguishable by the pale eye and fierce expression. Summer-plumage birds lose these flecks.

Pink legs

FLIGHT

Notice the smaller 'mirrors' than common gull (opposite).

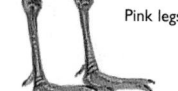

No flecks on head

Fierce expression

ADULT SUMMER HERRING GULL

FIRST WINTER

Smaller white spots ('mirrors') on wing-tips

35

Woodpigeon *Columba palumbus*

Few gardens will be without this, the largest pigeon in Britain, a frequent client on bird-tables or ground stations. Highly sociable birds, woodpigeons gather in great flocks in agricultural areas, greedily guzzling all sorts of crops and being a serious pest to farmers. Apart from grain, they are also partial to legume crops, such as clover. When disturbed, woodpigeons burst out of trees with a great clattering of wings, leaving a few feathers behind (all this is an intentional 'shock' ruse against predators). When identifying them, watch for groups of pigeons all looking the same; this will eliminate the feral pigeon, which always shows great plumage variation from bird to bird.

VOICE
Soothing, crooning song of five syllables, the second and third ones stressed: 'take TWOOO COOOS Taffy'. Heard all year.

WHERE FOUND
Abundant resident in farmland, woodland, cities and gardens. Big flocks move around in winter, some from the Continent.

IDENTIFICATION
Long-tailed. Pot-bellied, small-headed. Portly. Looks overweight and ungainly as it waddles over ground. White wing/elbow patch. Pale edgings to main flight feathers (primaries).

Lemon-yellow eye

White neck-ring

ADULT

YOUNG

No white neck-ring

YOUNG
Lacks white neck-ring. Darker eyes. Can be seen in almost any month, mostly early autumn.

FLIGHT
Direct, with continual flapping. Note diagnostic white crescents across the wings, found on no other pigeon species. Stock dove is smaller, wings lack white crescents, shorter tail. Grey centres to wings.

White wing crescents

Long-tailed

Grey centres to wings

WOODPIGEON

STOCK DOVE

DISPLAY

In display flight, rises up to a point, claps its wings, then glides down. Also claps its wings in level flight. Upon landing, spreads tail then slowly raises it, as if almost overbalancing.

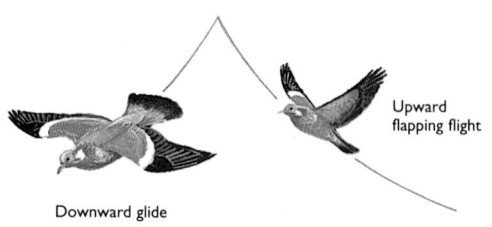

Upward flapping flight

Downward glide

DRINKING

Pigeons are among the few birds which can suck water up, rather than tilting their heads up to let gravity do the work.

Wing stretched in bathing

GARDEN TIPS

Woodpigeons need little encouragement and will feed on almost anything. Most foraging is done on the ground although birds will also use bird-tables. Cypresses are often selected as nest-sites, particularly early in the year.

RAIN-BATHING

Woodpigeons make a comical sight as they arch one outspread wing after another over the back, to expose their 'armpits' to the rain.

BREEDING

Pigeons are extraordinarily productive birds that breed whenever food is available, in any month of the year. The stick nest, usually built on the branch of a tree, is often so flimsily constructed that the eggs can be seen through it from below. The clutch is always two, and this holds good for all pigeons and doves. The squabs (young pigeons) are fed on a special 'pigeon milk', manufactured in the crop.

37

Feral pigeon *Columba livia*

If you have a town or city garden, this will be 'just another pigeon', a somewhat annoying visitor to the bird-table as it scatters smaller birds by its sheer bulk. This is the bird familiar from Trafalgar Square, the bird that lives in both seedy buildings and palaces, an inhabitant of dark alleys and coastal cliffs. It has a reputation for being a messy, scatty bird; where plentiful, pigeons can be a health hazard. Every feral pigeon seems to look slightly different. Colours range from reddish to white to black, with all kinds of markings; shapes also vary, from streamlined racing pigeons to the ornamental fantail pigeon. But they are all descended from the same species, which has long been domesticated.

VOICE
Quiet voice familiar from birds displaying shamelessly in town parks: a throaty, broody stammer 'look-at-the-MOOON'.

WHERE FOUND
Widespread resident in built up areas. Less of a farmland bird than woodpigeon. Ubiquitous in cities.

VARIETY
Most individuals show some grey, and many have iridescent purple-green neck marking. Variety is usual in feral pigeons; in flocks of other pigeon species, individuals look much the same.

Smaller than woodpigeon, heavy

Paler grey wings and back

Green neck patch

Eyes red

Large, plump

White neck patch

White on wings

Eyes yellow

Eyes black

Green neck-ring

Slim, small-headed

FERAL PIGEON ('wild rock dove type')

WOODPIGEON

STOCK DOVE

Dark lines on upperwing

FLIGHT

Flying feral pigeons often show two dark lines on the inner part of the hindwing. Many also show a white rump, absent in other species. Smaller and somewhat slimmer than the woodpigeon, with longer wings noticeable in flight. It flies even more rapidly than its relative.

White rump

DISPLAY FLIGHT

In display, birds flap slowly, then glide on wings held in a V-shape.

V-shape

HOMING

A multicoloured flock of racing or homing pigeons in flight. Famed for their ability to navigate, pigeons are known to use several clues to find their way home: the sun, landmarks on the ground, the earth's magnetic field and even their sense of smell.

Ruffled neck feathers

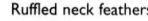

DISPLAY

On the ground they spread their tails, ruffle their neck feathers, and coo coaxingly.

NEST

For a nest-site, feral pigeons prefer a sheltered ledge on a building or natural site.

They also nest in holes, eg, in dove-cotes (this is the origin of the term 'pigeon-hole'). They usually nest in colonies, laying two white eggs. Anyone starting a dove-cote might need a special pair introduced to attract others.

Stock dove *Columba oenas*

Not a well-known bird, easily overlooked because of its similarity to other grey pigeons (despite the name, there's no real difference between a 'dove' and a 'pigeon'). This species is shyer than its commoner relatives, and it less frequently feeds at peoples' feet or on garden bird-tables. Like the woodpigeon, it shows a consistency of plumage not found in feral pigeons. On the ground, look for the green neck-ring (no white), subtle pink breast, black spots on the wing (which merge to form bars) and dark eyes. Although plump, it looks delicate. In flight it looks more compact than other pigeons, with shorter wings and tail; the wing-beats are softer, less powerful, sometimes flickering. Overall, it takes some experience to distinguish this bird, which suffers from the unfavourable impression given by its unruly relatives!

MORNING VISITS
Stock doves usually visit bird-tables early in the morning, and prefer tables some distance from the house.

Dark eyes

Green neck-ring

VOICE
Makes a pleasant, simple cooing 'oo-w-oo', uttered in series; the first note is stressed, giving overall a rather disapproving tone.

Grey centres to wings

Black bars on wing

WHERE FOUND
A resident, common in farmland and woodland throughout most of Britain.

FLIGHT PATTERN
In flight, look for the black-bordered grey wing-panel – quite distinct from the woodpigeon's white flashes (see page 36).

GARDEN TIPS

Feeds on grain, leaves and shoots. Stock doves nest in outbuildings and also use nest-boxes with a 20 cm (8 in) in diameter.

PAIRS

Stock doves are usually seen in pairs, being less sociable than other pigeons. Look for the understated display flight in a wide circle around the trees, in which both of the pair take part.

NEST

Unlike woodpigeons, stock doves nest in holes, most often in trees·but also in buildings. Occasionally they use rabbit burrows! They can be encouraged to use boxes, but suffer competition from tawny owls, which add insult to injury by eating them!

BREEDING

Where undisturbed, stock doves are as productive as other members of their family, sometimes rearing five broods in a season.

The clutch is always of two eggs, and the young are reared on 'pigeon milk' made in the gullet of both sexes. This nutritious food, rich in fat and protein, is similar in composition to mammalian milk. Among birds, only pigeons, flamingoes and penguins are known to produce it.

41

Collared dove *Streptopelia decaocta*

In some places, the collared dove seems to adorn every roof and aerial, filling the neighbourhood with its soft cooing. This is the smallest, slimmest common garden pigeon, and much the palest, with an all-over creamy wash. It shows very little contrast in the plumage. Where the collared dove is present it is hard to miss, being happier than other pigeons to feed on bird-tables, and conspicuously using high perches from which to launch its sailing display flight. Mostly seen in pairs or small groups, collared doves do nonetheless form flocks, especially around favoured feeding sites such as poultry farms or granaries. When fleeing, it has a typical pigeon over-reaction, with much panicky flapping.

VOICE
When it lands, it raises its tail up slowly, and almost always utters a loud series of buzzy whines, like roll-up party trumpets. The song – delightful to some, infuriating to others – is a constantly repeated chant 'un-i-ted', with the middle syllable the longest. It can form a constant backdrop to some suburban atmospheres.

IDENTIFICATION
Seen close to, the collared dove shows some subtlety in its plumage: pale grey cap and inner edge of wing, warmer brown on the mantle and back, white edges to the tail. Appears pale, especially on the head and neck. Single black neck-ring distinguishes from all other pigeons.

Pale grey cap

Black neck-ring

SIMILAR SPECIES
Compare the size and build to the feral pigeon and woodpigeon, the other common garden species. Occasionally collared doves are confused with the domestic Barbary dove, which is even paler.

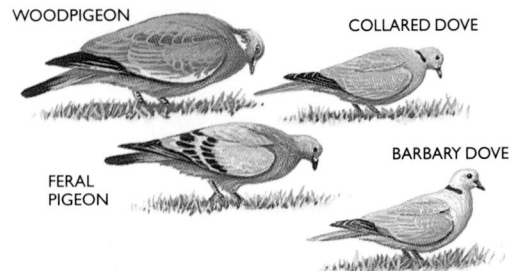

WOODPIGEON

COLLARED DOVE

FERAL PIGEON

BARBARY DOVE

DISPLAY

A common sight is the display, in which birds rise up and sail on spread wings and tail. Notice the dark inner part of the tail from below.

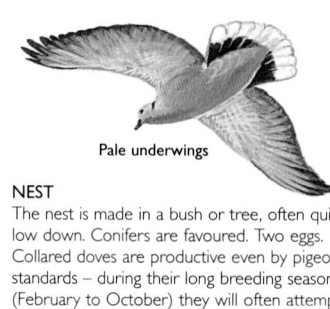

Pale underwings

NEST

The nest is made in a bush or tree, often quite low down. Conifers are favoured. Two eggs. Collared doves are productive even by pigeon standards – during their long breeding season (February to October) they will often attempt four or five broods. One pair tried nine!

White edges to tail

Like other pigeons, collared doves raise their tails on landing, lowering them slowly. When they do this, listen for the 'party trumpet' calls.

Swept-back wings

WHERE FOUND

Common widespread resident. Was never seen in Britain before the 1950s. First pair bred in 1955, now over 250,000 pairs.

FLIGHT

A very definite flicking action, on swept-back wings. This feature can pick them out at a great distance (but beware of confusion with turtle dove, page 44). Other pigeons have a much more steady wing-flap.

Turtle dove *Streptopelia turtur*

Spring sees the arrival of turtle doves in the countryside and into larger rural gardens. Attractive and popular birds, they are often detected by their delightful, soporific song, a lazy purring which gives rise to the name 'tur-tur'. To many birdwatchers, this song evokes hot summer days. The turtle dove is slimmer than all other doves or pigeons, with a fast, agile flight, tilting from side to side. It has a unique combination of intricately scalloped plumage and a zebra crossing' neck-ring. This species feeds mainly on weed seeds gathered from the ground; sometimes small groups also gather in areas where grain is spilled, for example in farmyards. Rarely can they be encouraged to visit bird-tables.

WHERE FOUND

It breeds mainly in south-east England. A migrant, arriving in April and leaving in September.

IDENTIFICATION

Turtle doves and collared doves are close relatives. Here they feed side by side on spilled grain. Turtle dove: smaller size, scalloped plumage. Unique black-and-white neck-ring. Red eyes.

COLLARED DOVE

TURTLE DOVE
Scalloped plumage

Red eyes

Black-and-white neck-ring

FLIGHT

Turtle doves fly amazingly fast. Look for the rapid, flicking wing-beats, and dark underwings contrasting with pale belly. There is less contrast in the collared dove.

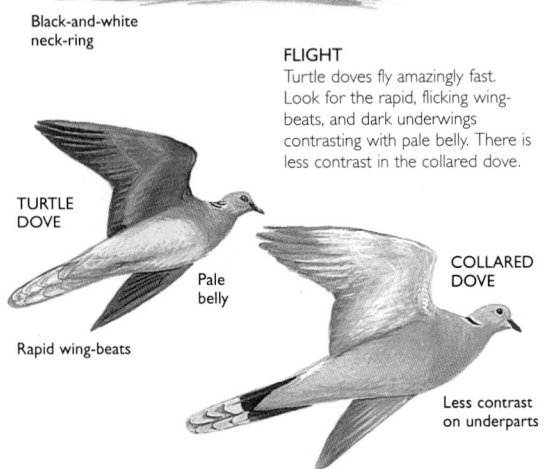

TURTLE DOVE

Pale belly

Rapid wing-beats

COLLARED DOVE

Less contrast on underparts

GARDEN TIPS
Does not really use bird-tables but might feed on grain on the ground. Turtle doves nest in hedgerows or gardens near arable fields. They may also use isolated large shrubs or conifers.

PERCHING
Often seen perching on overhead wires, turtle doves are usually seen in ones or twos. When landing, the white 'necklace' at the end of the tail stands out.

White tail 'necklace'

DISPLAY
A regular feature of pair-formation and maintenance in pigeons is mutual preening, or 'allopreening'.

Mutual preening

No neck-ring

YOUNG

YOUNG
Juvenile turtle doves lack the neck-ring of adults.

BREEDING
The clutch of two eggs is typical of pigeons. Being migrants, turtle doves have less time to be productive than others in their family, and normally only manage two broods. The nest is hidden away in dense bushes, especially of hawthorn or blackthorn. The species winters in West Africa. On their way, many thousands are shot for sport, especially in France. For this reason, turtle doves tend to be extremely wary.

Ring-necked parakeet *Psittacula krameri*

This bird is an incongruous sight as it flies noisily overhead or competes with starlings and sparrows for scraps on the bird-table. 'What's a parrot doing flying wild in Britain?' is most people's reaction when they first see a parakeet in the wild. It never looks part of the British countryside, but is slowly establishing itself, especially in the Home Counties, after being introduced in the 1960s. A regular user of bird-tables in gardens, it is probably dependent on them for its survival. It also visits hanging feeders for seeds and nuts, where it can be quite aggressive when necessary – it's armed with the sort of bill that can end arguments! Although brightly coloured and easy to see in the open, individuals simply melt away among green leaves and boughs. It roosts communally, and is generally sociable except when breeding.

WHERE FOUND
A resident species, currently commonest in the London area, but expanding its range.

VOICE
Constant loud, shrill piercing screeches; sounds a little like green woodpecker.

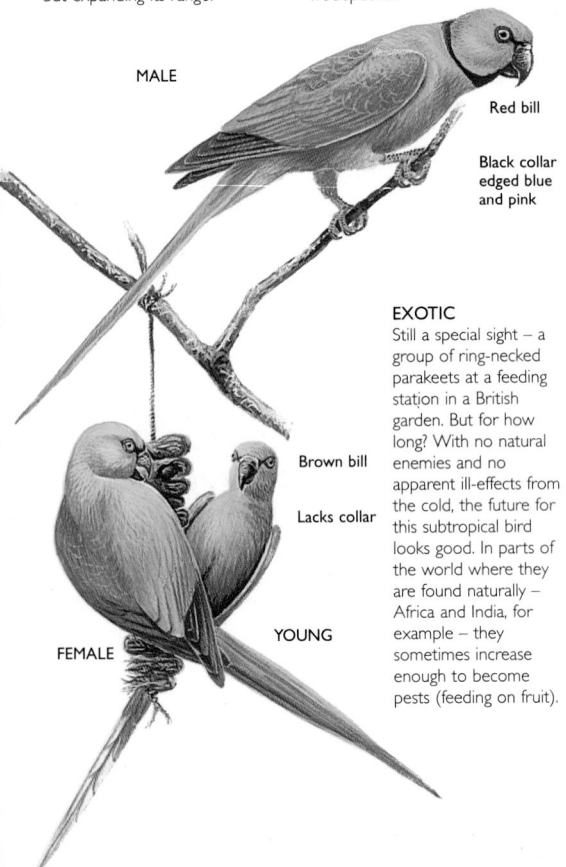

MALE

Red bill

Black collar edged blue and pink

Brown bill

Lacks collar

FEMALE

YOUNG

EXOTIC
Still a special sight – a group of ring-necked parakeets at a feeding station in a British garden. But for how long? With no natural enemies and no apparent ill-effects from the cold, the future for this subtropical bird looks good. In parts of the world where they are found naturally – Africa and India, for example – they sometimes increase enough to become pests (feeding on fruit).

FLIGHT

In flight, the rapid action on stiffly held wings looks like a small bird of prey, but the tail is much longer. Birds move very fast, with lightning changes of direction. Mostly encountered in flocks.

Rapid wing-beats

Stiff wings

NEST

Tree-holes in competition with starlings, woodpeckers and jackdaws. A clutch of two eggs is laid. Surprisingly, ring-necked parakeets have been found nesting in most months of the year, even in January, with no apparent loss from cold. Evidently, when they are well fed and suitably sheltered, the British climate is to their liking. Competition from other birds appears to be the main brake on their progress towards further establishment.

COCKATIEL

Grey plumage

Yellow face

OTHER ESCAPES

A few other exotic parrots occasionally escape and might be seen flying free in Britain. A prime example is the Cockatiel *Nymphicus hollandicus*, from Australia, which has a similar shape, but is grey with pale yellow on the face and wings.

GARDEN TIPS

Ring-necked parakeets are omnivores, but they love fruit, especially exotic fruit! They nest in holes in trees, but will sometimes use nest-boxes, competing for them with jackdaws and starlings.

47

Cuckoo *Cuculus canorus*

Known to all for its unmistakable, far-carrying call, the cuckoo is a popular herald of summer. It's very shy, and far more often heard than seen. Occasionally it may be observed perching on the tops of trees or on wires, but the best chance to see one is in flight. Look for the pointed wings and long tail, and, diagnostically, note that the wings never rise above horizontal when in level flight, so requiring a rapid, whirring beat. The shape and colour tends to recall a bird of prey: the narrow pointed wings and long tail of a kestrel, the grey and barred plumage of a male sparrowhawk. Perhaps youngsters are most likely to be seen in gardens, fussed over by their overworked foster parents; they are browner are more barred than adults. All ages can be mobbed by smaller birds, especially in the early breeding season. Cuckoos are particularly active at dawn and dusk, at least vocally.

VOICE
Males vary their 'cuckoo' song at any time to give a three-note version, and cough angrily in display. They don't actually 'change their tune in June'. Females give a startling, bubbling trill that is completely different.

WHERE FOUND
Very widespread. Present in summer (April onwards); adults leave in August, juveniles later.

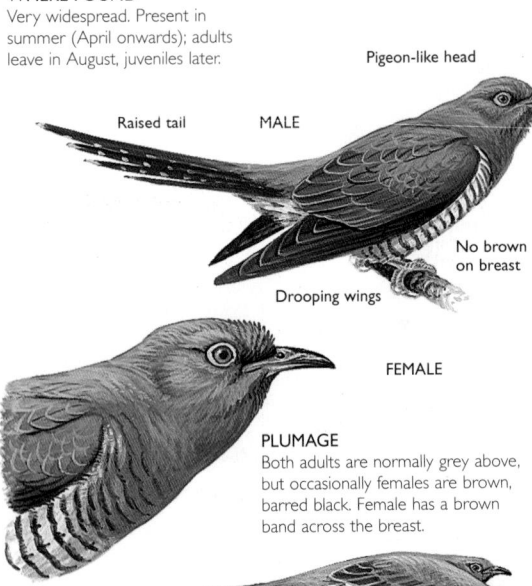

Pigeon-like head

Raised tail   MALE

No brown on breast

Drooping wings

FEMALE

PLUMAGE
Both adults are normally grey above, but occasionally females are brown, barred black. Female has a brown band across the breast.

FLIGHT
Wings are not raised above horizontal. Commonly calls in flight, especially during regular territorial beat around favoured calling perches.

Shallow wing-beat

EGG-LAYING

The cuckoo lays its eggs in other birds' nests. Each female lays up to 15 eggs, which mimic those of the host in size and sometimes colour. Females spend much of each spring day watching nesting activity around them, planning a raid. Each host nest is visited once; one egg is laid, one

host egg removed. Hosts lay in the morning, the cuckoo in the afternoon. Evidence suggests that a female lays in the nest of the species that raised her.

HATCHING

After hatching, the young cuckoo pushes rest of host's brood out of the nest. The fast-growing cuckoo gains sole attention from the foster parents. It soon dwarfs both nest and parents, but remains dependent even after leaving the nest.

Dunnock host

HOSTS

Dunnocks are favourite hosts, but other species are parasitised.

YOUNG

Juvenile cuckoos feed on hairy caterpillars in autumn, which are gathered from the ground.

JUVENILE

49

Tawny owl *Strix aluca*

Everyone knows an owl, with its large head, round face and huge, inquisitive eyes. The tawny owl is the commonest owl in gardens over most of Britain, and is the only owl species that regularly penetrates city centres and suburbs. All it needs is a few large trees, with holes in which it can nest. Nocturnal, it detects prey by sight and sound in almost total darkness, taking a wide variety of live prey, including small mammals and birds. These exciting birds are usually seen by luck, especially when the loud mobbing of small birds gives away their whereabouts. (Listen for the irritable 'chinking' of blackbirds; this is usually in response to an owl or a cat.) The richly patterned, brown plumage is ideal camouflage against a tree trunk. The sexes are alike.

WHERE FOUND
Widespread resident, absent from Ireland.
The tawny is the commonest owl in
Britain's gardens.

EYESIGHT
The forward-pointing eyes are
large, allowing in more light.
The view from each eye
overlaps with the other
('binocular vision'), so
owls can see an object
from two slightly
different angles,
which is especially
good for judging
distance.

Black
eyes

Rich brown
colour

FLIGHT
The rounded wings and bulky
body give a distinctive flight profile,
even in silhouette. The wing-beats
are slow, light and silent. The
feathers are specially adapted for
noiseless flight, which prevents the
prey hearing the approaching
predator, and helps the owl to
hear its quarry moving around.

Slow, silent flight

Rounded wings

BEING MOBBED

Roosting owls are sometimes discovered by small songbirds during the day, and harassed mercilessly with unwelcome noise!

VOICE

Very vocal at night, especially in autumn. Males give atmospheric hoot sequence: 'hooo…(four-second gap), hu-huhu-hoooo'. Both sexes also give sharp 'ke-WICK'.

NESTING

Tawny owls breed very early (eggs in March), so they can catch plenty of small mammals for their chicks before the vegetation grows up and conceals the prey. Up to four or five young may be raised, but this depends on the availability of rodents. The fluffy-feathered young leave the nest looking lost and are dependent on the parents for many weeks.

Owl pellet

PELLETS

A sure sign of an owl's presence, pellets are coughed up regularly. They contain bones and other indigestible remains of prey.

GARDEN TIPS

Takes readily to large owl nest-boxes. These should be cleaned out at end of the breeding season. Do not disturb nesting birds, for your own safety.

51

Little owl *Athene noctua*

Only the size of a mistle thrush, the little owl is tiny in compared to its relative the tawny owl, and is sometimes caught and eaten by it. It's more a bird of open country, requiring low turf or bare ground on which to catch its prey. Gardens next to fields are most likely to have it. Little owls should be looked for on fence posts, walls or ruins, or in isolated trees, tight to the trunk. The camouflage seems particularly suited to willow trees, on which it is often found. Unlike tawny owl, the little owl is frequently active during daylight hours, so it's far more often seen by birdwatchers than its larger relative. Even so, it still prefers to hunt around dusk or dawn for large insects, small mammals, small birds and worms.

VOICE
From autumn to late spring, the male gives a rather mournful hoot, upwardly inflected (downwardly inflected in tawny), and both sexes give a mewing 'kiew' used in all kinds of situations, sometimes in duet.

WHERE FOUND
Resident in England, Wales (scarce) and extreme south of Scotland only. Not native, having been introduced 150 years ago from the near Continent. It is mostly seen in farmland areas.

White eyebrow

Yellow eyes

Pale spotting

Head-bobbing action

IDENTIFICATION
Half the size of tawny, with white eyebrows and yellow eyes, the little owl should be unmistakable if well-seen. Look also for the pale spotting above. Little owls often bob their heads and bodies when alarmed or while hunting. It helps them to judge distance accurately.

GARDEN TIPS

Little owls nest in ruins and neglected buildings, so it's best to leave these undisturbed in little owl areas. Will also make use of conventional nest-boxes, although special 'hollow branch' designs are more successful.

HUNTING

The main hunting method to watch for is movement from a low perch, then dive down, talons first, on to the prey. The talons are widely spread to prevent escape. Hops on ground to hunt smaller prey.

Small size

Diving onto small prey

Hopping to catch prey

Striking 'eye pattern'

ANTI-PREDATOR TRICK

Eyes in the back of the head! The markings on the nape give the impression of eyes. This is probably a protective device, assuring a predator that it has been seen.

Undulating flight

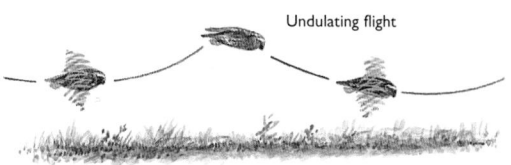

FLIGHT

Little owls are very distinctive in flight, as they bound up and down, with intermittent bursts of wing-beats. This undulating flight is similar to that of both the green woodpecker and the mistle thrush, species that occur in the same habitats and, given a poor view, might cause confusion.

53

Swift *Apus apus*

Swifts are always aloft. Parties sweep in long arcs over the rooftops, filling the summer skies with their piercing screams. This, the most aerial of all birds, spends most of its time flying, feeding on minute insects and web-transported spiders that float in the air. They will also feed low, especially in dull weather and when aquatic insect larvae are hatching over water. Swifts are best identified by their body-and-wing shape, variously described as scythe-like, or scimitar- or sickle-shaped. They often fly very high, higher than their aerial rivals the swallows and house martins. Late in the evening, parties of swifts disappear into the sky. (Many spend the night aloft, catching short snatches of sleep.)

WHERE FOUND
Widespread summer bird over most of Britain. Arrives from Africa in late April and leaves in August.

IDENTIFICATION
Looks all-black against the sky, but is actually dark brown with a tiny white throat-patch.

URBAN SOUNDS
Small groups typically fly around rooftops. Flight is accompanied by much screaming, an integral part of the swift's social system.

Dark brown colour – looks black

Long, swept-back wings

Small white throat-patch

Forked tail

Flickering flight

FLIGHT
Virtually always seen in flight and demonstrably masters of it, swifts are adapted for manoeuvrability. Despite the name, they are not particularly fast-flying. Flight is with flickering wing-beats or on long, sweeping glides. The wings are narrow, held out stiffly; the tail is forked, quite long, but frequently held so as to make the fork appear invisible.

Feeding

Preening

LIFE IN THE SKIES
Here, swifts demonstrate a range of aerial skills – feeding, drinking, preening and mating on the wing.

Mating

Drinking

NESTING

Swifts almost always nest in buildings, usually more than 10 m (33 ft) off the ground, and often much higher. They frequently nest in colonies. Church towers are favourite sites, especially in small villages with few tall buildings. The nest is made on a flat surface, often under the eaves of a house. Straw, grass and feathers are woven together with saliva. Swifts usually lay two eggs, three in good (warm and sunny) years.

HATCHING

The eggs hatch two days apart; this favours the older bird, which then gets the pick of the parents' offerings, often to the detriment of the other.

GARDEN TIPS

Readily takes to special swift nest-boxes, but the entrance must be blocked until the birds arrive in spring in case resident birds use the box first. A hole in the eaves may suffice instead of a box. Swifts prefer to nest in colonies. Beware when inspecting the nest, as it may be riddled with blood-sucking parasites.

Kingfisher *Alcedo atthis*

Quite a few owners of ponds begrudge losing their fish to herons, but no-one has such feelings for kingfishers. Tiny, dashing, jewel-like, bursting with bright colours and charisma, these gorgeous birds are always welcome. They are surprisingly small – sparrow-sized – with large heads, short tails and large, dagger-like bills (typical of fishing birds). That's if you see them of course, but usually they fly so fast over rivers and ponds that they have come and gone before you can draw breath. They can still be surprisingly difficult to see when perched; the orange blends into the sandy banks of the streamside. Don't be fooled by blue debris on the riverbanks, either! When nervous, kingfishers bob up and down, the tail wagging in time as if connected by a string. Obviously, gardens backing on to streams or rivers are most likely to have them, but individuals will pay a visit to garden ponds stocked with plenty of fish.

WHERE FOUND
This is a bird of still or slow-flowing water only. It is resident in most of Britain, but is very scarce in Scotland, where many of the rivers are too fast-flowing.

FEEDING
An unmistakable bird, the kingfisher waits patiently above the garden pond, in search of goldfish. Eventually it will plunge in head first and, if successful, might beat its capture on the perch before swallowing it.

PLUMAGE
Males have all-dark bills, while females almost always have some orange on their bills, especially at the base.

MALE

All-dark bill

FEMALE

Orange base to bill

Typically whirring flight

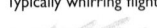

FLIGHT
The most common view of a kingfisher – dashing very low and straight over the water; on whirring wings. Note the especially brilliant blue back and rump.

DISPLAY

Pairs perform a delightful fish-presenting display in the spring; the male presents the gift, and the female takes it if she approves. Fish are swallowed head-first.

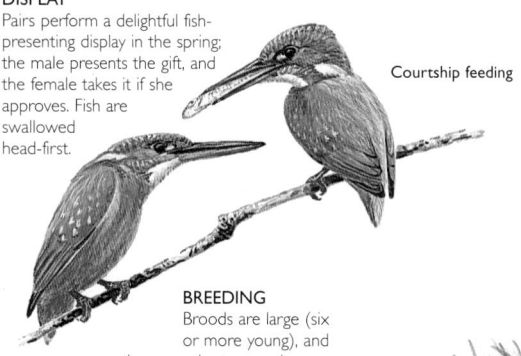

Courtship feeding

BREEDING

Broods are large (six or more young), and there may be two or three broods in a year. The young have a rota to ensure equal distribution of food, each bird taking its turn to face the entrance. Youngsters look duller than their parents.

NEST

The nest is excavated by both birds in a sandy bank. The tunnel may be more than 1.2 m (4 ft) long, with a chamber at the end. Holes in occupation can often be detected by the white excreta below the entrance.

Young leaving the nest

VOICE

A distinctive shrill call, like a dog whistle, and with a similar pitch to squeaking car brakes.

GARDEN TIPS

Will nest in artificial tunnels and banks. Often visits garden ponds in search of fish and frogs. Dig and hope!

Green woodpecker *Picus viridis*

This exciting bird, by far the largest of woodpeckers, invariably makes a spectacular sight. It's usually seen in flight first, when its presence is given away by its brilliant yellow rump. Then it lands on the trunk of a tree with a final upward sweep and suddenly becomes motionless, disappearing. It will cling to the reverse side of the trunk from an observer, and pop its head round every so often to keep watch. The green wash all over its body provides deceptive camouflage among green leaves and green-stained trunks. The green woodpecker's favourite food is ants, so it prefers to come to gardens with a reasonable area of lawn.

WHERE FOUND
Resident, absent from Ireland and less common in Scotland. Mostly inhabits areas with mature deciduous trees.

VOICE
Loud, ringing laugh, slightly accelerating, called 'yaffling'.

IDENTIFICATION
Has green body, paler on the underside, and is often seen feeding on the ground. Has a black face with a red crown and staring white eyes.

Red crown

White eye

Green body

Red moustache

Pale underside

MALE

All-black moustache

FEMALE

BILL
The powerful bill can excavate holes, but green woodpeckers don't 'drum' like other woodpeckers.

Stiff tail

FLIGHT
Yellow rump conspicuous from behind. Flight is up and down, bounding, the bird closing its wings every three or four beats. Beware of comparably-sized mistle thrush and little owl, which follow similar pattern. Mistle thrush, in particular, may also cause confusion on ground, looking almost yellowish in bright light.

Bounding flight

Yellow rump

DISPLAY
Males in territorial encounter face each other and sway from side to side.

NESTING
Excavates its own nest-hole, like all woodpeckers. Tends to select a high site. The single brood of five to seven young takes a terrible toll on the local ant populations.

YOUNG
Young are characteristically spotted, but still have green wash on back.

YOUNG

FEEDING
Green woodpeckers may feed on the ground for hours, if they find a rich food source, such as an ant colony. They lap the ants up with their long tongues.

Spotted underparts

GARDEN TIPS
Green woodpeckers will visit bird-tables in large gardens, usually early in the morning, to eat suet, mealworms and bird cake. They will use large, enclosed boxes with a 6.3 cm (2½ in) hole. The box must be at least 38 cm (15 in) deep and placed high up. Wood chippings should be provided as nesting material.

59

Great spotted woodpecker *Dendrocopos major*

This is the commonest woodpecker in gardens, and is intermediate in size between the larger green woodpecker and the smaller lesser spotted woodpecker. All woodpeckers cling to vertical trunks, resting on their stiffened tails, and move up and down (but mostly up) with heavy, ungainly hops. The sharp, powerful bill is used for searching in wood for food, for excavating nesting and roosting holes, and for drumming, a quite distinct activity, where the bill is beaten rapidly against wood to make a territorial sound. This is really the 'song'. Some great spotted woodpeckers have been known to use inappropriate sounding-boards on which to drum, such as drainpipes and aluminium ladders! This species is becoming more and more frequently seen in suburban gardens.

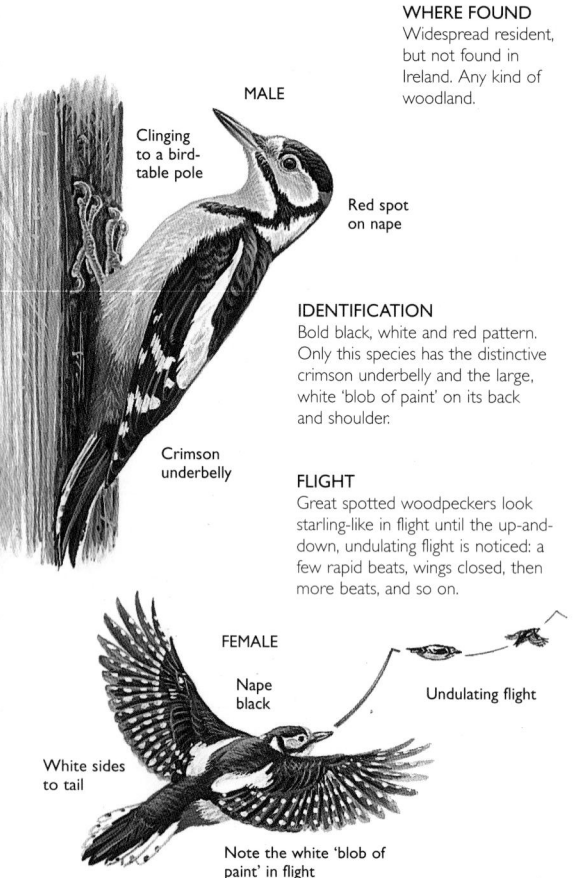

WHERE FOUND
Widespread resident, but not found in Ireland. Any kind of woodland.

MALE

Clinging to a bird-table pole

Red spot on nape

IDENTIFICATION
Bold black, white and red pattern. Only this species has the distinctive crimson underbelly and the large, white 'blob of paint' on its back and shoulder.

Crimson underbelly

FLIGHT
Great spotted woodpeckers look starling-like in flight until the up-and-down, undulating flight is noticed: a few rapid beats, wings closed, then more beats, and so on.

FEMALE

Nape black

Undulating flight

White sides to tail

Note the white 'blob of paint' in flight

GARDEN TIPS

Loves peanuts, suet, fat and oats, but this shy visitor is easily disturbed. Nests in enclosed boxes, with 5 cm (2 in) entrance hole, 30 cm (12 in) deep. Place the box high and fill with chippings. Predates nestlings of other birds, hammering through nest-boxes with its bill. Use a metal plate to protect the entrance.

Red vent

Nest excavation

FEEDING

Commonly seen clinging to peanut bags, as here. Usually only one individual will dominate the garden scene, as territories – held by both sexes separately in the winter – are large.

NESTING

A great spotted woodpecker excavating its nest, expelling wood chips. Both sexes do this. Like many other activities, it is accompanied by a common, explosive 'chip' or 'tchick' call, also used in alarm.

Complete red crown

YOUNG

Pink vent

YOUNG

Show a full red crown and a pale pink vent. Beware of similarity to male lesser spotted woodpecker (see page 62), which is nevertheless much smaller.

61

Lesser spotted woodpecker *Dendrocopos minor*

An appropriate name for this uncommon and amazingly elusive species might be 'less spotted'. Comparable in size to a sparrow, it is a woodpecker in miniature. Its movements are dynamic and brisk; its flight is light and fluttering. It feeds briskly, usually on the topmost and outermost branches of trees, particularly favouring small trees with weaker bark, such as alders, willows, birches and fruit trees. Some individuals wander, and may turn up unexpectedly, adding to the charisma of this generally unfamiliar bird. A privilege for any garden!

VOICE
A remarkably quiet bird, adding to the difficulties of detecting it. Male makes an excited peeping, fairly similar to green woodpecker's laugh, but all on one note and less ringing. Drums, especially early morning February to May; drumming quieter and more even than great spotted.

WHERE FOUND
Very uncommon resident, not in Scotland or Ireland.

MALE

Short bill

FEMALE

White crown

Black nape

Red crown and nape

Larger bill

GREAT SPOTTED WOODPECKER

Larger size

IDENTIFICATION
Lesser spotted woodpeckers are small with short bills. The breast is streaked, the vent white with some streaks. Males have a red crown and a red nape.

SIMILAR SPECIES
Great spotted woodpeckers are larger, with longer, more powerful bills. They have a 'splodge' of white on the back, a red vent and a black crown. Males have a red nape.

LESSER

'Ladder back'

GREAT

White patches

FLIGHT
Note the lesser spotted's 'ladder back' — white horizontal stripes down the back. Smaller size.

Tail
held off
branch

Stiff tail

SILHOUETTE
Beware the similar-
sized nuthatch (left),
which never presses
its tail to the trunk as
a woodpecker does.

FEEDING
Lesser spotteds usually feed
on outermost branches and
twigs, unlike the great
spotted, which sticks to
trunks and larger boughs.
The `smaller species moves
rapidly from tree to tree,
but will also settle for long
periods in a favoured spot.
It is more insectivorous than
the larger species.

Moth-like
display flight

DISPLAY
Lucky observers
occasionally witness
this bird's fluttering,
moth-like display
flight, which includes
much chasing.

YOUNG
Similar to female. The
young male shows a
small amount of red
on the crown.

YOUNG

GARDEN TIPS
Scarce and shy visitor to bird-tables, mostly in early morning. Eats
nuts and suet. Position any nest-box high on the underside of a
branch. Box should be enclosed, with an entrance of 3 cm (1½ in)
and a depth of 30 cm (12 in). Fill with wood chippings .

Swallow *Hirundo rustica*

F ew birds are more closely associated with the passing of the seasons than the fair-weather swallow, the bird of summer. Its return in spring is eagerly anticipated: will the same pair come back to nest in the garage roof or the garden shed? It's unthinkable that they shouldn't. The swallow feeds over fields and nests in low buildings, so it is commonly found in rural areas, especially farmland. This is one of three common British garden birds to live a highly aerial lifestyle; the others are the house martin and the swift. The swallow is always easily distinguished by its long, deeply forked tail.

IDENTIFICATION

Adults are glossy royal blue above and cream below. They show a red-chestnut throat, bordered by a blue breast-band. Juveniles are duller, especially on the throat, and have much shorter tails. The throat is orange brown rather than red chestnut.

VOICE

Pleasant twittering, rambling song, often with buzzes, in flight or perched, eg, on a wire. In alarm or excitement, utters a chirp like a sparrow's, but somewhat more cheerful.

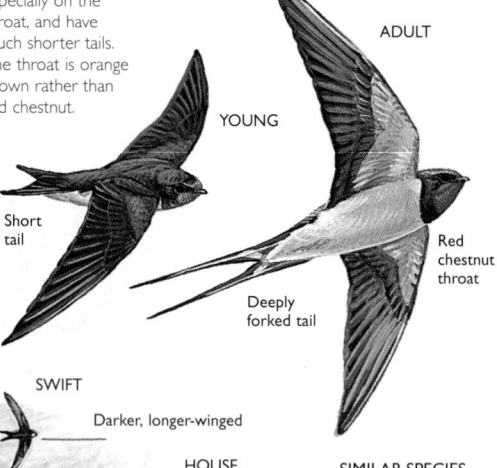

ADULT

YOUNG

Short tail

Red chestnut throat

Deeply forked tail

SWIFT

Darker, longer-winged

HOUSE MARTIN

High flight

SIMILAR SPECIES

The house martin is less attenuated and has a white rump and a haphazard flightpath, often flying higher than swallows. Swifts are darker and longer-winged, and fly in long, high sweeps.

FLIGHT

Low in long, straight sweeps with graceful glides. Flies lower still for larger prey, such as blowflies.

SWALLOW

Low flight

WHERE FOUND

A summer visitor, arriving in early April and often not leaving until October (juveniles); very common and widespread.

WATER

Often feeds over water; also skims low enough to take a few sips. Frequently uses garden ponds.

NESTING

Selects farm buildings, sheds and garages for nesting, so long as there is permanent access (a small slit will do).

BREEDING

If possible, swallows return to the same site every year. The nest is constructed of mud and grass, and is sited on a beam or rafter, usually close to the roof. Females select their mate on the length and symmetry of his tail streamers: long, equal ones are deemed best. Pairs often have two or three broods in a season.

YOUNG

Waiting for parent to arrive with food

A restless autumn flock waiting to migrate

GARDEN TIPS

Swallows will feed in gardens with fields or open countryside nearby. A garden pond will provide food, and also mud for the nest. They can be encouraged to nest by placing a shelf on a low beam in a disused building or outhouse, but need a permanent access point, so leave a window or door open.

House martin *Delichon urbica*

House martins are familiar from their habit of making mud-nests under the eaves of houses. The comings and goings of small colonies have hooked many a casual watcher. Like the swallow and swift, house martins are highly aerial. They fly around in short, wheeling glides with frequent turns, more slowly than the swallow and swift and appearing less direct, more rambling. If anything, a house martin seems to know its limitations, it doesn't try to be clever, just forages at a moderate height for the many flying insects that fill our skies in summer.

VOICE

The call is an enthusiastic though rather gravelly and spluttering 'prrt'. The song, a twittering elaboration of this, is heard from the nest.

WHERE FOUND

A summer visitor, arriving in April and departing in October. Common and widespread in countryside and some suburbs, it is always found near habitation.

SIMILAR SPECIES

The swift has long, stiff, narrow wings, all-dark plumage and a moderate tail fork. The swallow has longish, swept-back wings and a deeply forked tail.

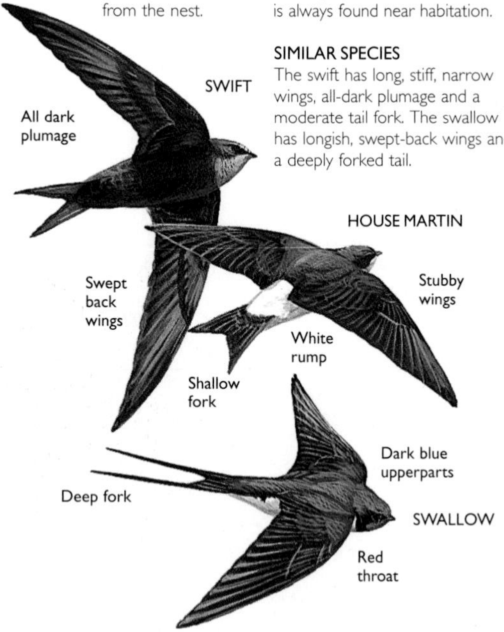

SWIFT

All dark plumage

HOUSE MARTIN

Swept back wings

Stubby wings

White rump

Shallow fork

Dark blue upperparts

Deep fork

SWALLOW

Red throat

ADULT

JUVENILE

IDENTIFICATION

House martins have dark blue upperparts, clean white underparts and white rumps. The wings are stubby and the tail has a shallow fork. Male and female look alike. Juvenile (seen here sat next to an adult) looks browner and dingier than the adult.

NEST BUILDING

Arriving in spring, house martins waste no time in constructing their nests. The first stage is to collect mud of different consistencies from the ground: garden ponds are ideal for this. At such times their white-feathered legs can be seen well.

Collecting mud

Feathered legs

COLONY

A typical colony, with much activity – prospecting and feeding flights to and fro, minor squabbles, begging young. More nests are attempted than are finished and used. Most pairs try two or three broods during a season. A busy colony generates plenty of noise, and a good deal of mess below it.

GARDEN TIPS

You can't provide food for house martins, but they often hunt over large garden ponds and may take mud for their nests. Will nest in colonies under the eaves of houses. If you don't have nesting birds you can encourage them by providing several specially made house martin nests (available commercially), but there should be a colony nearby that can supply pioneering birds. Affix the nest-boxes under eaves, or under a shelf fixed to the wall. The entrance hole should be 2.5 cm (1 in) wide only, to exclude sparrows.

Pied wagtail *Motacilla alba*

An expert in the art of tail-wagging, 'wagtail' is an appropriate name for this bird. Its tail could move up and down in its sleep, and probably does! These birds spend much time searching for insects on lawns, fields or roadsides, paying little regard to the presence of human activity. Normally moving with a deliberate gait, they will speed up and run extremely fast when pursuing a choice meal. At other times, they will just as quickly leap into the air and chase after a flying insect. Often they perch on roofs, which make ideal look-out posts and are good places for insects if facing the sun. In the breeding season, wagtails are most likely to be found near a river or pond where insects are plentiful. Almost any garden, however, whether mostly grass or concrete, will probably be visited at some time.

WHERE FOUND

A common, widespread resident, found in many habitats.

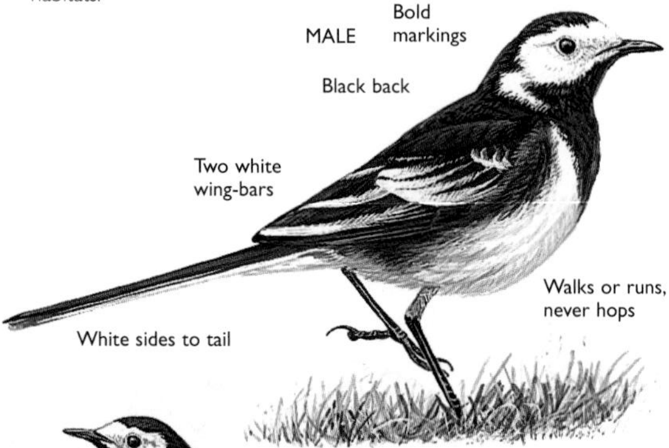

Head bobs as it walks

Bold markings

MALE

Black back

Two white wing-bars

White sides to tail

Walks or runs, never hops

Dark grey back

FEMALE

Often less black on head and breast

Long claws

Winter plumage

IDENTIFICATION

Pied wagtails have a complicated set of plumages. In summer, both male and female have a smart black throat and upper breast. In winter, they strip down to a mere narrow breast-band.

VOICE

Shrill but gravely 'tschizzik'. The male has a rambling song based on this call.

Exaggeratedly up-and-down (undulating) flight

NEST

This bird nests in many different places. The basic requirement is a ledge with a small amount of shelter – a hollow where a brick has fallen from a wall, the eaves of a farm outbuilding, a riverbank, the tangled stems of a creeper – it could be anywhere. An open-cup nest is carefully constructed of grass, roots, moss and hair, which will provide a home for five or six nestlings.

YOUNG

Young pied wagtails further complicate an already complicated picture. They lack the smart plumage of their parents, tending to look brownish-grey and often have a distinct yellowish wash to the head and breast. There is only a small amount of black on the breast.

YOUNG

Yellowish wash to head and breast

ROOSTING

In winter, these birds often roost together in large numbers – sometimes hundreds. Look for them in urban streets and glasshouses.

GARDEN TIPS

Sometimes comes for scraps on bird-tables. Struts around on lawns looking for insect prey. Will use open-fronted nest-boxes and usually nests in undisturbed outbuildings, sheds and machinery. Finding a nest can be a good excuse to do less gardening.

69

Grey wagtail *Motacilla cinerea*

Don't be confused by the name 'grey', because this bird's most eye-catching feature is its lemon-yellow coloration on the breast, rump and undertail (only the back is grey). Unfortunately, the name 'yellow wagtail' belongs to another species (see opposite). The grey wagtail is really a bird of rivers, especially fast-flowing streams in hilly areas, but it wanders quite freely in winter to visit a variety of watery areas, including gardens with ponds. Here, it will seek static and flying insects, moving along with the familiar wagtail walk and skip, working both the lawn and the immediate edges of the water.

WHERE FOUND
The grey wagtail is widely distributed in Britain and Ireland, and is present throughout the year.

VOICE
The call is sweet (less harsh than pied wagtail). 'Tzi-zit' rather than 'tschizzik'. Song is a series of slow, insect-like trills.

SUMMER PLUMAGE
Predominantly yellow below and grey above. Lacks bold black-and-white of pied wagtail.

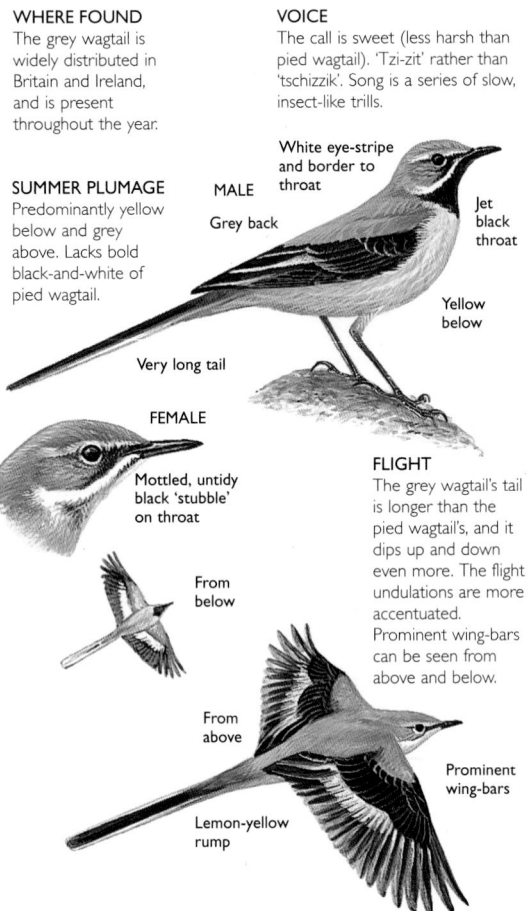

White eye-stripe and border to throat

MALE

Grey back

Jet black throat

Yellow below

Very long tail

FEMALE

Mottled, untidy black 'stubble' on throat

From below

FLIGHT
The grey wagtail's tail is longer than the pied wagtail's, and it dips up and down even more. The flight undulations are more accentuated. Prominent wing-bars can be seen from above and below.

From above

Prominent wing-bars

Lemon-yellow rump

WINTER PLUMAGE
A winter-plumage grey wagtail feeds by a garden pond. In winter, it has a pure white throat and loses most of its yellow coloration, except around the tail.

White throat

TAIL-WAGGING
The grey wagtail wags its tail even more than the pied wagtail, but why all this tail-wagging? It could be to make them look more conspicuous to one another. It could be to disturb, or attract, flying insects as they forage. It has even been suggested that the tail wags in time with plants moving in a river, creating a kind of camouflage. No-one really knows.

NESTING
Grey wagtails usually nest close to water, on a ledge with some shelter. One or two clutches of four to six eggs are laid. When the young leave the nest, they are virtually tail-less, but they still wag their rear ends.

YELLOW WAGTAIL
This related species may occur in gardens. A summer visitor from April to September. Distinctive 'sweep' call.

Yellow head

Green back

Shorter tail

YELLOW WAGTAIL

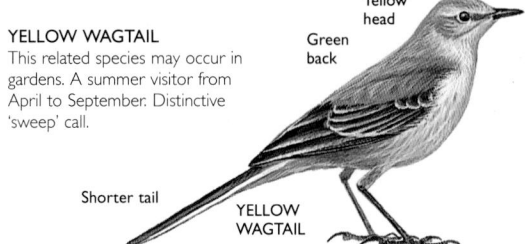

GARDEN TIPS
Grey wagtails are not great users of feeding stations, but they like to forage around garden ponds. If you have a river in your garden or nearby, grey wagtails may nest in suitable open-fronted nest-boxes or on platforms. (They are particularly fond of nesting under bridges.)

Waxwing *Bombycilla garrulus*

When small groups of this rare, exotic winter visitor adorn berry-laden shrubs and trees in suburban and urban streets, even non-birdwatching members of the public stop and stare, while the birds feed at a few metres' distance, oblivious to all around them. The waxwing's true home is the far north, among the shrubs and coniferous trees of the 'taiga' belt, so when they make their occasional visits to Britain they are probably encountering people for the first time. Although most of our visitors feed in hedgerows, many soon discover 'berried treasure' in gardens. Such is the waxwing's charisma that some wildlife gardeners plant berry-bearing shrubs especially to attract them, and may be rewarded with a visit only many years later.

IDENTIFICATION
With its crest, soft pinkish plumage, and red-and-yellow markings on the wings and tail, the waxwing poses no identification problems. In general shape and size it resembles a starling.

VOICE
In flight, waxwings give a very distinctive call, a silvery trill recalling a pea-whistle.

Group of waxwings on berry crop, together with starlings and thrushes

FEEDING
The winter diet is almost entirely berries, but waxwings do eat other fruit as well. In summer, they seem to subsist on mosquitoes, which they catch in acrobatic flycatching sallies.

WHERE FOUND
'Irruptions' occur when a very good breeding season for the birds has coincided with a very poor rowan berry crop in Scandinavia. In good years (approximately once every 20 years), flocks can be scattered throughout Britain from October to March.

FLIGHT

This is whirring, like a starling's, on similarly triangular wings, but is a little more buoyant, and slightly more undulating.

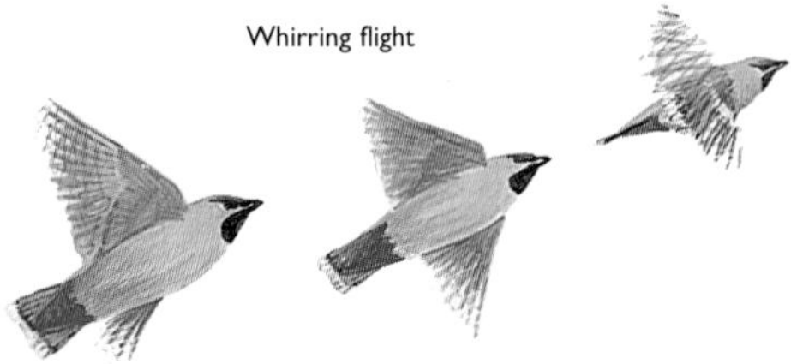

Whirring flight

ADULT MALE

Waxy red tips on wings

PLUMAGE

Males are slightly brighter coloured than females, with more waxy red tips on the wings and a cleaner black throat. First winter birds are distinguished by their wing pattern; the adult's yellow 'V' on the tips of its primaries is replaced by a line.

FIRST WINTER

No yellow 'V' on primaries

GARDEN TIPS

May visit a garden if there are berry bushes present. Plant a berry-bearing shrub – cotoneaster, hawthorn, pyracantha, rowan – and wait for the next waxwing invasion.

Waxwings feeding acrobatically

Wren *Troglodytes troglodytes*

The tiny wren looks shorter than any bird, with its tail held cocked up in perky fashion. It is very common, but, because of its small size and love of thick, tangled undergrowth, is seen much less often than many garden birds. Sometimes it will perch for a short time on a fence, bobbing up and down and flicking its tail, and then depart on rapidly whirring wings to its next destination, always appearing hurried. The name 'Troglodytes' means 'cave-dweller', referring to its life lived among the secret passageways of apparently impenetrable ground vegetation. Every so often it leaves its hideaway to announce its presence with incredibly loud bursts of song, or to display irritation at a rival or predator by bouts of 'tek-tek' calls. It makes up for its size by its effervescence.

FEEDING

With patience, wrens can be observed feeding on or near the ground, where they hop and creep along in search of smaller insects and spiders. Watch for the bobbing action, flicking tail and general restlessness.

PLUMAGE

Mostly brown, dark above, light below. Copious barring around wings. Long, slightly curved bill. Pale brown eyebrow, giving inquisitive expression. Male and female look alike.

Pale brown eyebrow

Brown upperparts

VOICE

The song is an out-burst of over 100 notes, shrill but musically liquid and always with a trill near the end. It is sung all year round, even in mid-winter.

Pale underparts

Male in song

WHERE FOUND

Our most numerous resident bird; found wherever there is ground cover.

NEST

In early spring, the male starts to build a series of nests from moss and leaves. It will often build four or five 'cock-nests' and sometimes up to ten, but will make only the outside structure of each, leaving them unlined. By a special display the male presents its work to a local female, which registers approval by mating. Then the female adds the lining to the structure of its choice, so completing the nest.

Moss-gathering for nest

BREEDING

The nest is domed, with the extra covering necessary to keep the tiny chicks insulated. The lining of hair and feathers also helps. The nest is placed in cracks or crevices in walls or among foliage, especially creepers. Two broods of five or six young are raised.

GARDEN TIPS

Wrens will come to bird-tables to feed on breadcrumbs and mealworms. Being very small, they suffer particularly in cold winters. On winter nights, they sometimes roost together, huddled in small shelters, closely stacked on top of each other to keep warm. Up to 60 have been recorded in one nest-box! Wrens will also roost in houses and outbuildings. They make their nests in a variety of places, such as creepers, woodpiles, walls and old coat pockets!

75

Dunnock *Prunella modularis*

Formerly called the hedge sparrow, and often confused with sparrows, this is the archetypal small brown bird. It's actually quite distinctive by virtue of its shape and actions – especially in the way it creeps quietly over the ground, and in the regular and almost mechanical flicking or shivering of its wings – but it will never cast away its superficial appearance of 'just another sparrow'. The dunnock is a very common bird which inhabits the majority of gardens. It visits bird-tables, but prefers to remain on the ground, on the hunt for small seeds and, in the breeding season especially, insects. Much of its foraging takes place under cover of flower borders or hedgerows, which is in keeping with this bird's unobtrusive character.

WHERE FOUND
Very common resident, less numerous in Scotland.

BEHAVIOUR
Dunnocks shuffle along the ground, intermittently flicking their wings – an old country name was 'shufflewing'. This behaviour sets them apart from most other species.

Dark streaking

DUNNOCK

Thin bill

Greyish wash

FEMALE HOUSE SPARROW

IDENTIFICATION
Dunnocks have a greyish wash over the head and breast, and attractive streaking on the wings, back and flanks. Thin bill. Pink legs and eyes. The female house sparrow has a thicker bill and obvious pale eyebrow.

VOICE
The song is a slightly repetitive warble which reminds many of a squeaky trolley. The call is a thin, piping 'tseep', like the opening of a squeaky iron gate.

DISPLAY
In spring, the wing-flicking becomes more earnest and focused. Rival males show their antagonism by 'wing-waving', a slower version of flicking, where both wings are raised at once or each is raised alternately.

Wing-waving display

PAIR-BONDING

The self-effacing dunnock has rece.., famous for its pair-bonding systems. This singing male dunnock will be a territory holder, possibly on its own, or possibly in co-operation with another, subordinate male. Where there are two males, there will usually be several females of equal status in the same territory. The inter-relationships are complex, but, broadly speaking, each male will copulate with each female, so that everybody has more than one mate. This is called 'polygynandry'.

'Squeaky trolley' song,

GARDEN TIPS

Dunnocks prefer to feed at ground stations, where they will eat crumbs, small seeds, suet and crushed peanuts. They do not nest in nest-boxes, favouring hedges. To make sure hedges are bushy, trim them regularly.

NESTING

When eventually they get round to nest building, dunnocks build cup nests, usually in hedges or bushes. The four to six eggs are a strikingly bright blue.

Pale eyebrow

YOUNG

YOUNG

Young dunnocks are more streaky than their parents, especially below. Sometimes a pale eyebrow is noticeable.

One of our commonest and most familiar garden residents, the robin is many people's favourite bird of all, which only goes to prove that looks are more important than character! This bird exudes charm in its typical upright, alert stance, its wholehearted bobbing up and down, its colourful orange-red breast (fluffed up in cold weather), and especially in its tameness towards man. But to its own kind, however, it is ruthless and aggressive. Many garden robins are killed by other robins and, even in the absence of physical aggression, tensions abound. Other birds are not spared, for the robin's main feeding technique of 'watch and pounce' demands a certain lack of disturbance around it, so intruders are chivvied away. A volatile character.

THE SEXES
Angle of brown on forehead breaking into the red of the face forms a 'U'-shape in males and a 'V'-shape in females.

WHERE FOUND
Widespread resident. found in gardens and woodlands.

'V'-shaped area of brown on forehead

FEMALE

'U'-shape angle of brown on forehead

MALE

'Watch and pounce' feeding method

FEEDING
Robins hop over lawns in search of insects and worms or, in 'watch and pounce' method, perch low down, watching the ground underneath for insect movement before pouncing. Recently-worked earth offers plenty of displaced invertebrates, which is why robins watch gardeners with such keen interest.

NESTING
Robins are famous for their unusual nest-sites, among them kettles, pockets of coats, tin cans, or even the skeleton of a dead cat! More usually they select a shallow depression on a bank, where they raise up to three broods of five to seven young. When they fledge, the young are distinctly spotted, showing their relationship to the thrushes.

Length 14 cm (5½ in)

FIGHTS

Robins squaring up to each other. In direct confrontation, ma..
their bodies so that the red of their breasts is shown to best effect. If
song or 'tik' calls fail to remove a challenger, displays like this
follow, and then fighting. When robins fight, they will
attempt to peck at the head and eyes of their rival.
Deaths are common.

Territorial
aggression

SONG

Robins sing all year; in the autumn
it's almost the only bird singing.
Clear, shrill notes rise and fall,
speeding up and slowing down,
with a rather sighing, melancholy
air. The robin also utters a 'tik, tik'
call. Males and females hold
autumn and winter territories,
and both sexes sing, which is
unusual in birds. At the end of the
year, females invade neighbouring
males' territories, initially meeting
resistance, then tolerance and
finally partnership. Females stop
singing, and breeding begins as
early as February.

GARDEN TIPS

Loves cheese, butter
and mealworms. Will
nest almost anywhere,
often using outbuildings
such as sheds. Try
putting out a standard
open-fronted nest-box,
or an old kettle.

YOUNG

Spotted
breast

Black redstart *Phoenicurus ochurus*

This bird is a real speciality of places that would seem to be unattractive to birds – derelict sites, urban areas, power stations and industrial wasteland. Only a few very urban gardens will be visited. In many ways the black redstart resembles a robin – in its upright stance, hopping progress over the ground, and overall shape and size. However, it can always be recognized by its chestnut-red rump and tail, the latter being regularly quivered, and by the overall drabness of its plumage, lacking any orange-red on the breast. It spends much of its time on the ground, feeding, sometimes also making brief flycatching sallies into the air, in the manner of many insect-eaters.

VOICE
A pleasing warbling introduction precedes a pause, then there's an ultra-fast jangle that resembles the sound of ball-bearings being rubbed together, or paper being screwed up. Unique! The very tops of buildings or machinery are selected as song-posts. Sometimes over 5000 songs are delivered during a single day, mostly at dawn. Some individuals also sing during the night.

WHERE FOUND
Very local and uncommon in Britain, mostly England. In breeding sites April to September; also a migrant and scarce winter visitor.

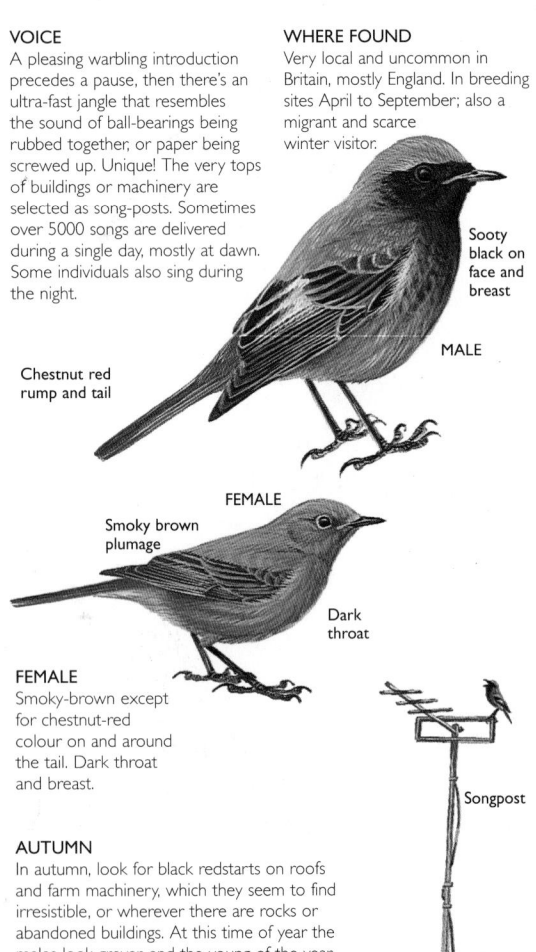

Sooty black on face and breast

MALE

Chestnut red rump and tail

FEMALE

Smoky brown plumage

Dark throat

FEMALE
Smoky-brown except for chestnut-red colour on and around the tail. Dark throat and breast.

Songpost

AUTUMN
In autumn, look for black redstarts on roofs and farm machinery, which they seem to find irresistible, or wherever there are rocks or abandoned buildings. At this time of year the males look greyer, and the young of the year have plumage similar to the adult female.

NEST

A pair chooses a ledge or hole in some suitable outbuilding or pile of rubble. Contrary to its surroundings, the nest is kept clean and tidy, undergoing a thorough spring-cleaning if it's to be used for a second brood. Four to six eggs are laid.

Chestnut-red tail obvious in flight

BREEDING MALE

Handsome; overall grey plumage intensifies to sooty black on the face and breast. Large white patch on the wing. Both sexes quiver their tails.

Look on roofs in autumn

White forehead

MALE REDSTART

FEMALE REDSTART

Pale throat

REDSTART

In the west and north, especially in woodland, look out for the redstart. Exclusively a summer visitor to Britain, from April to September. Also quivers tail. The female is similar to the female black redstart, but much paler brown, fading almost to white on the throat. The male has a unique combination of grey, black and red. White forehead.

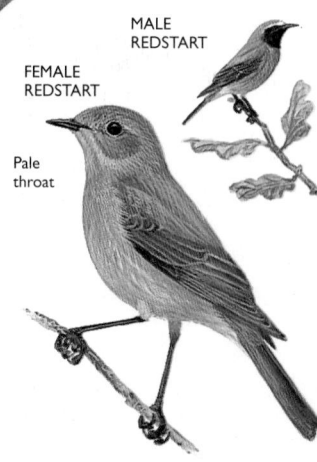

81

Blackbird *Turdus merula*

Consistently listed among the top five most common visitors to gardens, the blackbird must be familiar to every gardener, whether interested in birds or not. Few can fail to be moved by the glorious song, so much a feature of summer, and few could miss the birds as they run over our lawns in search of worms and insects. Typically, blackbirds run, then stop dead and put their heads on one side, apparently listening for movement; then suddenly a worm is pulled from the ground. They also have a habit of searching among leaf-litter, shuffling noisily with the feet or flicking items dismissively away with the bill. Generally, blackbirds are not very sociable, except at roosting time when nocturnal neighbours make irritable 'chink' calls at one another – a very familiar evening sound.

VOICE
Males defend territories in spring with a virtuoso song, effortless in delivery and low-pitched. Very relaxed and unhurried, there are pauses between each phrase, and every phrase is different. Older birds have more varied songs. Sings mainly February to July.

WHERE FOUND
Abundant, widespread resident. Also in woodland.

Dingy bill

FEMALE

Brown with some streaking

FLIGHT
When disturbed, blackbirds burst off with a noisy, panicky alarm rattle. Most flights are low, with a noticeably flicking wing-beat. When alighting, typically raise their tails and droop the wings.

Low flight with flicking wing-beats

JUVENILE

YOUNG
Just out of the nest, the copiously mottled juveniles resemble thrushes, but are darker and don't show black spots on the pale background of a song or mistle thrush. Young males in autumn are halfway between males and females in colour, but with a darker bill.

ALBINOS

Some individuals show varying degrees of white feathering (albinism). Occasionally the transformation is complete.

Partial albino

First winter bird

GARDEN TIPS

Blackbirds eat scraps – fat, cheese, sultanas and fruit (eg, apples) and prefer to feed on the ground. They love berries in autumn and winter. They will often nest in hedges and creepers and may use large, open-fronted nest-boxes.

Yellow bill and eye-ring

MALE

Jet black all over

SIMILAR SPECIES

Beware of superficially similar starling, which has different shape.

NEST

The nest is of grasses, leaves and moss, solidified with mud, with an inner lining of grass. Blackbirds have several broods a year, using a different nest for each brood. Early nests are often in evergreens, later ones usually in hedges, ivy, etc.

83

Fieldfare *Turdus pilaris*

This large, richly-coloured member of the thrush family visits us for the winter. Common on farmland from October onwards, it increasingly turns up in gardens as the season progresses, especially if the weather turns cold and snowy. It's a sociable bird, harvesting rowan and other berries in large, loose flocks, not just with its own kind but with other thrushes, too. Groups also hunt over pasture for invertebrates, including worms and leatherjackets, sometimes crossing fields step-by-step like an invading army. This bird is nomadic during the winter, so flocks can appear overnight in gardens. They will search lawns for invertebrates, but will be particularly grateful for berry-bearing bushes and thrown-out apples.

IDENTIFICATION
At first glance looks like any other thrush, but distinctive when seen well. Large compared to blackbird or mistle thrush. Grey head and rump, black tail, chestnut-purplish back and wings. White patch at base of wing. Yellow-and-black bill. Normally shy and unapproachable.

VOICE
Chattering, conversational 'chack-chack', the notes often running into each other.

Steel-grey head and rump

Chestnut-purple back and wings

Black tail

MALE

White underwings

FLIGHT
The fieldfare gives several flaps then closes its wings, giving rise to gentle undulations; the effect is rather leisurely. Here, a small flock is moving to a new feeding area. Flocks are disorganized and ragged.

GARDEN TIPS

Fieldfares visit gardens to eat fallen apples and other fruit, seeds or scraps. They prefer ground stations and will search lawns for invertebrates unless ground is frozen. Plant berry-bearing shrubs, eg, rowan and holly.

FEMALE

Less well-defined head and breast markings

FEEDING

Often flocks with other feeding thrushes, including redwing and mistle thrush. Fieldfares will feed on open, rough pastureland, whereas redwings prefer to be near cover. In wintry conditions fieldfares visit gardens for berries and fruit, sometimes using bird-tables.

MESSY DEFENCE

In Scandinavia, where the fieldfare breeds, the anxiousadults have an extraordinary way of deterring bird predators. Groups of fieldfares flyaround the intruder and pelt it with excreta, sometimes coating it so completely that it can no longer fly, and dies. Fortunately, they do this to people.

WHERE FOUND

Turns up commonly anywhere in Britain and Ireland, October to April more numerous in some years than others.

85

Song thrush *Turdus philomelos*

Midway between blackbird and starling in size, this is the most familiar 'spotty' thrush of our gardens, so often seen feeding quietly on the lawn, putting its head to one side and 'listening' for worms. Somewhat shy and retiring, it prefers to stay near the cover of borders or shrubbery, not out in the open. This species is quite at home in small gardens with plenty of undergrowth; the similar mistle thrush prefers large gardens in places where there's ready access to wide-open spaces. Famed for their songs, local males select high song-posts, such as aerials or tall trees, and dominate the neighbourhood with their vocal outpourings.

VOICE
A song of great beauty and inventiveness. Diagnostically, every word or phrase is repeated several times, at a studied pace. The call is a quiet 'tsip'.

WHERE FOUND
Widespread, common resident. Also woodlands, hedges.

SIMILAR SPECIES
In both species, the sexes are alike. The mistle thrush is loose-winged and -tailed, wings often drooping, pot-bellied, small-headed, with an upright stance. A pale bird, it resembles an anaemic song thrush. The song thrush is smaller, well-proportioned, sleek and neat. Warmer brown. Shorter tail.

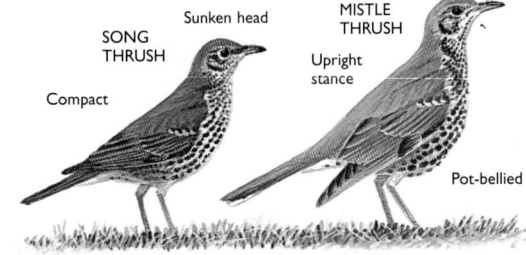

SONG THRUSH — Sunken head — Compact

MISTLE THRUSH — Upright stance — Pot-bellied

FLIGHT
Mistle thrush undulates up and down very strongly. Often flies some distance. Has white underwing. Song thrush has much lighter flight, usually short-distance, with less-pronounced undulations. Sandy-brown underwing.

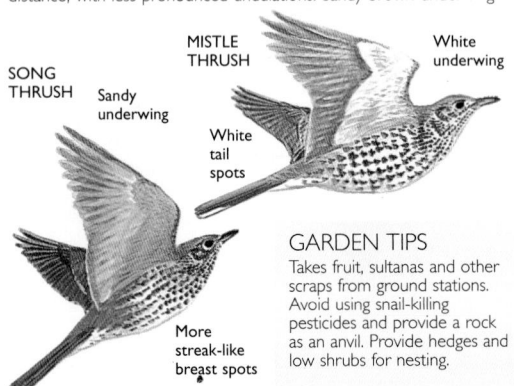

SONG THRUSH — Sandy underwing — More streak-like breast spots

MISTLE THRUSH — White underwing — White tail spots

GARDEN TIPS
Takes fruit, sultanas and other scraps from ground stations. Avoid using snail-killing pesticides and provide a rock as an anvil. Provide hedges and low shrubs for nesting.

SNAILS

A true sign of a song thrush's presence is an aggregation of broken snail-shells. Song thrushes have learned to dash the shells against a hard surface to break them open. A stone is the commonest 'anvil', but occasionally tree-roots have been chosen. One bird even tried a milk-bottle. Snails are mostly an emergency ration, bringing thrushes through times of harsh winter weather or summer drought. Blackbirds will readily steal the hard-won morsels if they get the opportunity.

Smashing snail
on 'anvil'

Blackbird stealing food

NEST

A favourite nest-site is a low shrub, such as a cypress. The grass nest has a mud (or dung) lining (in contrast to the blackbird's nest, which is made of sticks and mud with a grass lining). Three to five bluish eggs are laid, with a great variation in patterning.

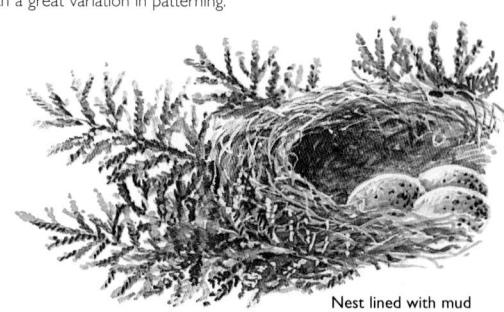

Nest lined with mud

Mistle thrush *Turdus viscivorus*

A big, powerful, often aggressive bird, surprisingly easy to overlook because of its similarity to the better-known song thrush. It is less common than the latter in gardens, needing wider areas on which to forage, and avoiding the dense patchwork of vegetation that makes up so much of suburbia. Pairs need plenty of space and nest relatively far apart – at such low densities, in fact, that the impression is of paranoia! Male mistle thrushes sing more in the late morning and afternoon than the other species, and they seem to be stimulated, not limited, by wind and rain – hence the country name 'storm cock'.

WHERE FOUND
Widespread resident. Also woodlands. Mistle thrushes often feed out in the open on pasture and playing-fields.

VOICE
Harsh 'football-rattle' call, which intensifies in alarm until almost deafening. Song: similar to the blackbird's, but more desolate-sounding, faster and with less variation; it tends to sound distant.

White tail-spots

Drooping wings

FLIGHT
A few flaps, then a close of the wings produces a very up-and-down flight, often low over the ground.

Bounding flight

White tail corners

NEST

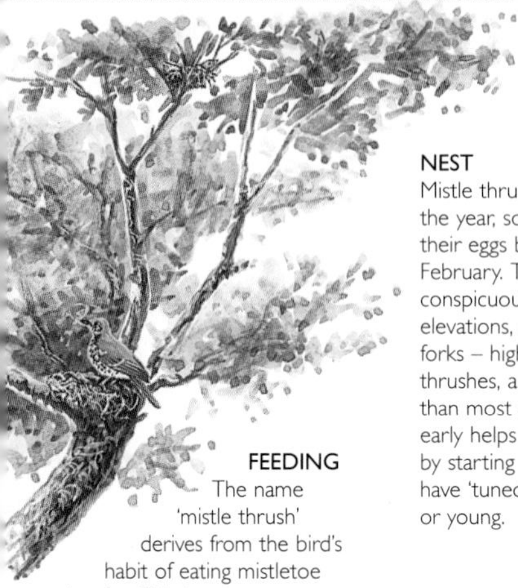

Mistle thrushes breed early in the year, sometimes laying their eggs before the end of February. They build large, conspicuous nests at high elevations, mainly in tree-forks – higher than the other thrushes, and indeed higher than most other birds. Nesting early helps avoid predation by starting before predators have 'tuned in' to finding eggs or young.

FEEDING

The name 'mistle thrush' derives from the bird's habit of eating mistletoe berries. This is a more developed trend on the Continent than in Britain. In autumn and winter, some individual mistle thrushes defend a feeding territory based around a clump of berry-bearing trees or bushes: rowan or holly, for example. The intention is to protect an exclusive winter food source, a kind of living larder, for the use of just one bird.

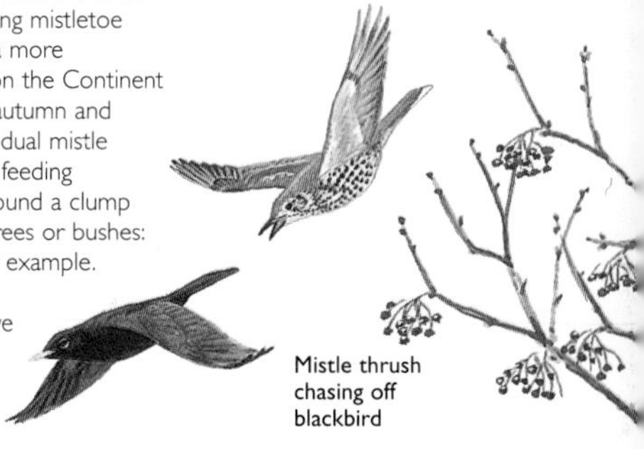

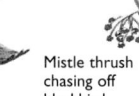

Mistle thrush chasing off blackbird

GARDEN TIPS

Mistle thrushes will come rather reluctantly to a bird-tables or ground stations for fruit, sultanas, etc. Plant holly, yew or rowan trees to supply them with berried food in winter. They need tall trees for nesting, and to provide them with elevated song-posts.

JUVENILE BLACKBIRD

Obvious spotting on back and head

JUVENILE MISTLE THRUSH

Similar to adult, but with obvious spotting on back. Paler and larger than blackbird

JUVENILE SONG THRUSH

Streaked on back

Warmer on breast than mistle thrush

Redwing *Turdus iliacus*

O n clear autumn nights, redwings travel on a broad front southwards and westwards, migrating away from Scandinavia to spend the winter with us, flying so low that their piercing 'tseeep' calls can readily be heard from the night sky. This atmospheric sound can be experienced anywhere, and is as much a sign of the seasons as the first swallow. The redwing is the smallest of the 'spotty' thrushes, similar in size and shape, in fact, to a starling. On the ground it is easy to recognize because, although superficially song thrush-like, it does stand out as pleasingly different. Throughout their stay, redwings are highly sociable, not just with their own kind, but also with other thrushes – particularly the fieldfare, another nomadic wanderer from the north. Together the two species are referred to as 'winter thrushes'.

WHERE FOUND
Redwings are widespread from October to April. Look in hedgerows and on farmland, They often visit gardens later in the winter.

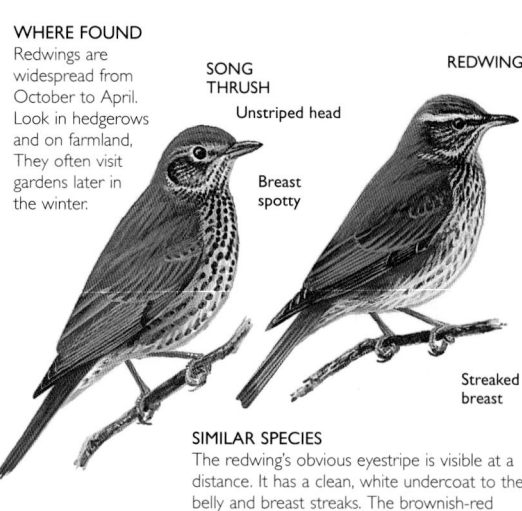

SONG THRUSH
Unstriped head

Breast spotty

REDWING

Streaked breast

SIMILAR SPECIES
The redwing's obvious eyestripe is visible at a distance. It has a clean, white undercoat to the belly and breast streaks. The brownish-red underwing leaks down onto the flanks.

Redwings on a playing field

VISITOR FROM ICELAND
This slightly larger redwing is darker and has more dense streaking on the breast.

FIRST WINTER
The redwings with pale edges to their wing feathers were hatched last summer.

FEEDING

Unlike their relative, the fieldfare, redwings are at home feeding on leaf-litter on woodland floors. They soon take to ground-feeding stations if seeds, scraps and fruit are provided. Although they are less addicted to berries than larger thrushes, redwings often take advantage of this highly nutritious, easily obtained food.

Redwings and starlings on hawthorn

FLOCKS

In early spring, flocks of redwings gather together and seem to 'chat' about the forthcoming migration back to their breeding grounds. The birds loaf around, just conversing, making a continuous excited babbling like an audience before curtain-up.

Obvious red underwing

FLIGHT

The flight is fast, and straight, not undulating, with regular slight changes in direction. Look out for the reddish underwing.

GARDEN TIPS

Redwings visit gardens when it is cold. All winter thrushes love soft fruit, especially fallen apples. Redwings prefer to take these from the ground, but they will visit bird-tables if times are hard. They will also eat grated cheese. Berry-bearing trees and bushes will attract redwings and other thrushes in winter.

Blackcap *Sylvia atricapilla*

Best known as a common summer migrant, the blackcap has become an increasingly frequent winter visitor to gardens in the last 30 years. While the bulk of the population moves southwards to spend the winter on the Mediterranean (what a good idea!), a few thousand mavericks remain with us from October to March, and mostly rely on the generosity of bird-gardeners to get them through hard times. Although fruit is a favourite food, they are omnivorous, and will take all kinds of kitchen scraps, from bread to fat. Recently, they've even taken to using peanut bags. Catch the blackcap trend – no garden should be without one!

WHERE FOUND
Blackcaps are common throughout Britain and Ireland in summer, and widespread but scarce in winter.

VOICE
The call is a sharp 'tak', similar to the wren's 'tek'. The song is a few mumbly notes that suddenly give way to a confident whistled tune of high quality, quite similar to an improved, extended robin phrase.

FIRST WINTER MALE

Slightly browner cap

ADULT MALE

Black cap

IDENTIFICATION
The clean-cut black skull-cap of the male gives the bird its name, but the female is equally distinctive with her reddish-brown version. Young males are somewhere in between.

BEHAVIOUR
Like all warblers, blackcaps are restless birds, seldom remaining still for long. They seem to disappear effortlessly into foliage, making short flights within bushes, and hurried, jerky flights between bushes. They will glean from leaves, hover after flying insects, and devour berries.

WINTER FEEDING

Here, a female blackcap feeds from a bird-table, showing off her chestnut-brown cap to advantage. Individuals that spend the winter in northern Europe are now known to be immigrants from the Continent, specifically northern and eastern Europe.

Chestnut cap

FEMALE BLACKCAP

SIMILAR SPECIES

The blackcap is slim and grey-brown. Note the thin warbler's beak. The marsh tit has a thicker head and more rounded body. It is a warmer brown and has whiter cheeks. Note the black bib and shorter, thicker bill.

MALE BLACKCAP

Thin bill

BREEDING

Mostly summer birds, blackcaps breed very commonly in woods and larger, bushy types of gardens.

MARSH TIT

GARDEN TIPS

Blackcaps will eat berries, eg, blackberries, rowan and holly. At the turn of year, they will visit bird-tables to feed on oats, bread, fruit and scraps. They also need thick bushes for foraging and roosting.

93

Chiffchaff *Phylloscopus collybita*

The chiffchaff could easily be overlooked but for its persistent, very singular song, from which it gets its name. A small, olive-green warbler, darker above and paler below, the blue tit-sized chifffchaff blends in among the green leaves of the summer canopy. Although they are mainly summer visitors, a few chiffchaffs remain to spend the winter with us. These birds often use gardens, and may visit bird-tables for scraps. They look small and fragile.

VOICE

'Chiff-chaff, chiff-chaff': the song is actually a random sequence of 'chiffs', 'chaffs' and 'cheffs', spoken in short sentences at a regular pace, like a metronome. In spring, males sing for their territory from a high perch.

WHERE FOUND

Apart from Scotland, the chiffchaff is a common summer visitor to deciduous woods and large gardens from March to October. It is a scarce winterer, mostly found in the south.

FEEDING

Active and restless like all warblers, the chiffchaff can be difficult to see well as it searches actively for invertebrates. It adopts the various postures it needs to glean the foliage effectively. The chiffchaff persistently dips down its tail when feeding.

Tail dipped when feeding

SONG

Chiffchaffs wag their tails when singing and seem fond of dead twigs as song-posts. This enables them to be seen properly. Their song is heard from early March; birdwatchers listen for it eagerly, as a sign of spring.

SIMILAR SPECIES

The chiffchaff and its relative the willow warbler are notoriously similar, causing endless problems to birdwatchers. The best distinction is the song, but there are plumage differences.

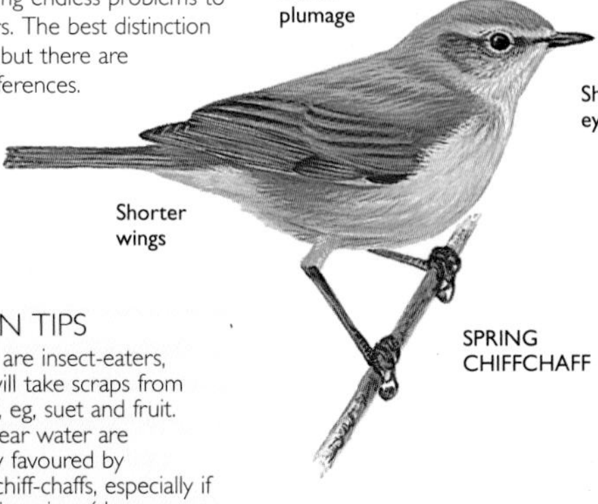

Duller plumage

Rounder head

Shorter eyebrow

Shorter wings

GARDEN TIPS

Chiffchaffs are insect-eaters, but they will take scraps from bird-tables, eg, suet and fruit. Gardens near water are particularly favoured by wintering chiff-chaffs, especially if the water is a river (damp areas provide a year-round insect supply for them).
Note: willow warblers don't overwinter in Britain or Ireland.

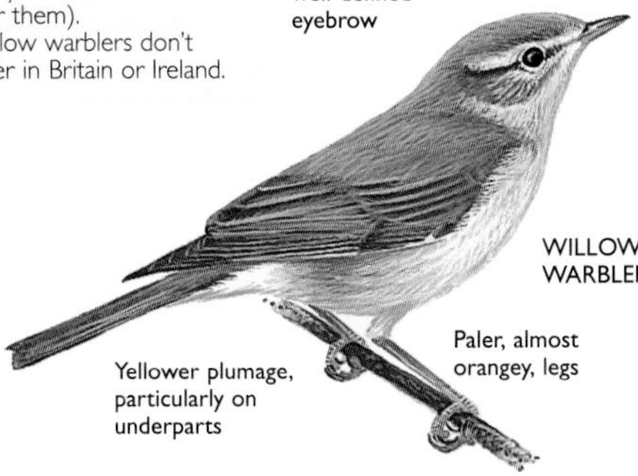

SPRING CHIFFCHAFF

Longer, more well-defined eyebrow

WILLOW WARBLER

Paler, almost orangey, legs

Yellower plumage, particularly on underparts

Using bird-table in winter

WINTER FEEDING

Like most small birds, a wintering chiffchaff must spend all the daylight hours feeding, if it is to survive the cold.

Willow warbler *Phylloscopus trochilus*

This is another leaf warbler, notoriously similar to the chiffchaff, and always causing confusion. Rather than saying 'chiff' or 'chaff', however, it sings a soft, whispering phrase, that goes gently down the scale. Perhaps more than any other, this song is a true sign of spring, since all our willow warblers retreat to tropical Africa for the winter and only return in late March and early April. The willow warbler is a very small, yellow-green bird with a thin bill. Like all warblers it is continually active, especially when foraging for insects, and it alternates its search among leaf surfaces with brief aerial flycatching sallies. In summer it lives in bushy areas and woodland edges, particularly birch, preferring quite open scrub rather than tall woodland favoured by the chiffchaff, the other so-called 'leaf warbler'.

WHERE FOUND
Widespread and very common from late March to October.

IDENTIFICATION
A small, yellow-green warbler, very similar to the chiffchaff (see opposite).

Singing chiffchaff

Singing willow warbler

SONG
Willow warblers almost always select lower song perches than chiffchaffs. Their song-phrase starts quietly, accelerates and gets slightly louder, then fades away at the end.

NESTING
Both leaf warblers forsake the tree-tops for nesting, placing a domed structure of grass, moss and leaves on the ground (willow warbler) or just above it in tangled vegetation (chiffchaff). There is a wide entrance to the side of the nest to allow a good view of possible danger. The willow warbler lays about six eggs that are whitish with light reddish-brown spots.

SIMILAR SPECIES

These are the plumages adopted by the birds after July. The willow warbler looks much yellower and cleaner than the chiffchaff. The eyebrow is even more distinct. Note the longer wings (for longer migration) and the paler legs.

No eye-ring

Obvious eye-ring

Longer wings

Paler legs

WILLOW WARBLER

Shorter wings

Darker legs

AUTUMN CHIFFCHAFF

GARDEN TIPS

Willow warblers are unlikely to come to bird-tables to feed. However, they will visit gardens that provide plenty of cover and the shrubs recommended to encourage insects (see page 11). This small bird takes some berries in the autumn. It breeds in many large gardens and is a common and widespread visitor on migration in the autumn.

Willow warblers foraging

CONTACT CALLS

Both willow warblers and chiffchaffs utter soft whistles: the willow warbler's is slightly mournful, and nearly two syllables, 'hoo-eet'; the chiffchaff's is a much more cheerful, upbeat 'hweet!', of nearly one syllable.

97

Goldcrest *Regulus regulus*

This is the smallest bird in Britain, even tinier than the wren, so it's easy to miss as it forages busily among needles in conifer trees. Look for it mostly in pines, spruces and cypresses, where it is always on the move probing for insects. Small groups of goldcrests often visit gardens in winter when they may feed lower down than usual, making use of a wider range of trees, so almost any garden is likely to receive a visit at some time during this season. Look for an active, tit-like shape without instantly obvious markings: the crown is only visible at reasonably close range.

IDENTIFICATION
Plumage dull-green, with pale bars on wings. Needle-thin bill separates it from the tit family. The male has orange on its crown, most intense near nape. This is especially evident in display, when the crown is raised. The female's crown is yellow.

VOICE
The call is tiny, intense and has ultra-high-pitched 'zee' notes, often in threes. The song consists of double notes building up to a flourish.

MALE

Orange crown

Needle-thin bill

Yellow crown

FEMALE

Dull-green plumage

WHERE FOUND
Common and widespread from October, when continental birds arrive to spend the winter.

FORAGING
Goldcrests never stop moving. They dart from branch to branch, constantly flicking wings and frequently hovering. Clusters of needles act as a barrier to snow, allowing them to forage in depths of winter. To keep alive, they must feed for 90% of daylight hours. After dark, they huddle together in small groups to keep warm.

NEST
Made of moss, woven with spiders' webs and lined with feathers that form a protecting rim at entrance. Almost always in a conifer, suspended from a small branch, often quite high up. Two broods of 10 young each are raised to combat the high mortality of such small birds.

Nest woven with spiders' webs

Forked tail

Double wing-bar

FLIGHT
Looks very weak, but goldcrests can cross the North Sea. Note the double wing-bar, forked tail and minute overall size.

ADAPTATIONS
Goldcrests have special ridges on their toes that help them cling to pine-needles in almost any acrobatic position.

GARDEN TIPS
Goldcrests will occasionally visit gardens to take crumbs and suet from bird-tables, and they will nest in any reasonably-sized conifer. The rare firecrest, however, would be a lucky find in any garden.

Bronze shoulder-patch

FIRECREST
The rare firecrest, *Regulus ignicapillus*, has a fresher and more sparkling plumage than the goldcrest. Note the black eye-stripe.

Pied flycatcher *Ficedula hypoleuca*

Flycatchers live up to their name, making regular darting flights on their long wings to catch insects, including flies, in mid-air. The smart pied flycatcher is the smaller of our two species, looking plumper and more compact than the spotted flycatcher. This dapper bird intersperses its rapid flycatching sallies with foraging in the treetops and on the ground. When perched, it regularly flicks its wings and tail, usually while giving a sharp 'chip' call. Mostly associated with sessile oakwoods, the provision of nest-boxes has helped it to spread south-eastwards from its traditional strongholds in the west and north. Where gardens back on to suitable habitat, it can be a welcome and familiar summer resident.

VOICE
The song is an even-paced 'scraping' phrase that rises and falls to no great tuneful effect. Often wags tail while singing.

WHERE FOUND
Mostly north and west, especially Wales, from April to August (leaves early on migration).

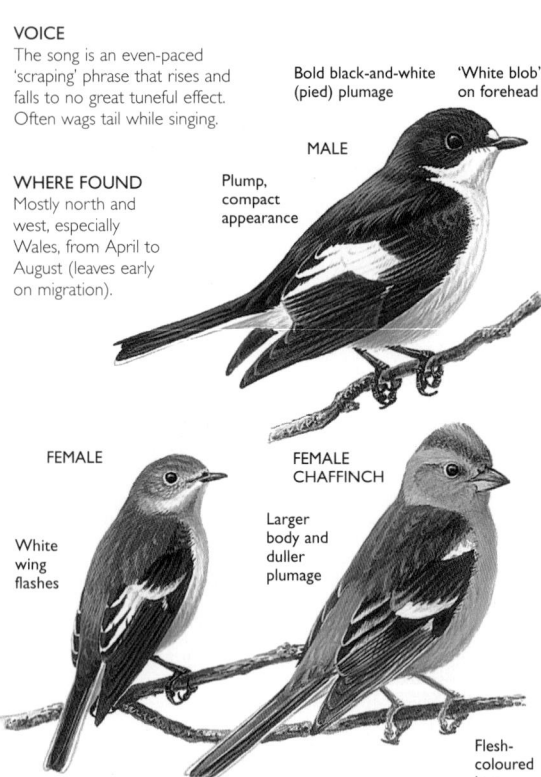

Bold black-and-white (pied) plumage

'White blob' on forehead

MALE

Plump, compact appearance

FEMALE

White wing flashes

FEMALE CHAFFINCH

Larger body and duller plumage

Flesh-coloured legs

IDENTIFICATION
Male pied flycatchers are unmistakable in their bold black-and-white (pied) plumage. The female is white below, but brown above, sharing the male's bright white wing-flashes. She generally appears much duller. Both sexes have black legs. The black coloration of the male fades as summer progresses and by autumn the sexes are barely distinguishable. A female chaffinch, found in similar habitats, might cause confusion. Note the chaffinch's thicker bill and head, longer tail and flesh-coloured legs.

FLYCATCHING

Note how pied flycatchers change perch between flights to catch insects. The spotted flycatcher often returns to the same perch.

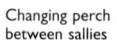

Changing perch between sallies

Nest-showing display

DISPLAY

Singing from the roof of a nest-box is part of the 'nest-showing display' given in the presence of a female.

BREEDING

Pied flycatchers are often polygynous (the male has more than one mate). It is an act of deception, because the females have no knowledge of each other – the territories are some distance apart. A clutch of five to eight eggs is normal.

An adult brings in a caterpillar

GARDEN TIPS

Pied flycatchers will use an enclosed nest-box with a hol_ of up to 5 cm (2 in) in diameter. Make sure th_ perch within _ easy access_ with tits, so _ until the flyca

YOUNG

Once they've left the nest, the young are fed for longer than most fledglings. They have mottled, scaly plumage.

Spotted flycatcher *Muscicapa striata*

The garden environment is very much to the spotted flycatcher's liking. We provide plenty of prominent perches for these birds to sit on, and we plant flowery borders to attract hordes of insects for them to eat. Pairs readily adopt open-fronted nest-boxes, and build nests among ivy or other creepers. In return, they show little fear of us, and can be easy to watch. The spotted flycatcher has large eyes, a flat bill with wide gape (to catch insects), a long tail and very long wings. It is a bird of high summer, arriving late in May and not breeding until June. This is when its favourite food – large flies, bees, wasps and butterflies – is most abundant. Despite its name, it is not spotted at all (except when young).

VOICE
The male arrives before the female and sings a poor, unmusical, disjointed song that is difficult to hear. Far more typical is the main call – a brisk 'whiss-chk'.

WHERE FOUND
Spotted flycatchers are widespread from May to September.

Large eyes

IDENTIFICATION
Male and female are alike, unlike the pied flycatcher. Plumage is plain grey-brown above and paler below with streaking on the breast and crown. (There are no spots at all.) They choose prominent perches to sit on.

Plain grey-brown plumage

Streaky breast

Calls from a prominent perch

GROUND FEEDING
Visits to the ground are uncommon. A flycatcher feeding like this is probably hampered from its normal foraging by bad weather. Strong winds are the main problem.

FLYCATCHING

The spotted flycatcher perches upright on a prominent perch, silently and still, then rapidly darts in any direction to catch prey in flight. Often returns to the same perch, in contrast to pied flycatcher, which usually changes perch.

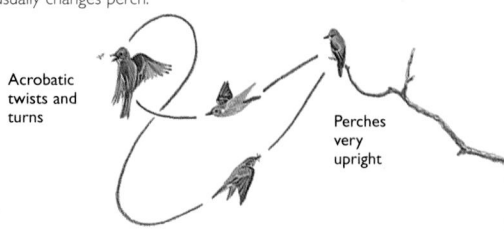

Acrobatic twists and turns

Perches very upright

GARDEN TIPS

Spotted flycatchers feed on butterflies and other insects that are attracted to flowers, so plant many flowering species. Buddleia is particularly recommended. They will nest in open-fronted nest-boxes if you place boxes low, among foliage. Will also nest in creepers.

NESTING

The spotted flycatcher is almost always monogamous. The pair selects from a variety of sites, such as tree-holes, ivy, wall crevices, or even a kettle or letter-box.

YOUNG

Spotted plumage

FEEDING YOUNG

Caterpillars must be beaten to death first (they could bite the chicks); bee and wasp stings must be removed.

YOUNG

Fledgling spotted flycatchers are spotted. As they grow into juveniles, they resemble adults but have stronger pale lines and spots on the wings.

103

Long-tailed tit *Aegithalos caudatus*

Long-tailed tits are always seen in flocks apart from a short period in spring, when pairs separate into territories. When foraging, these birds never stop moving. Individuals are busy, flicking tails-and performing acrobatics. Groups pass quickly from tree to tree or bush to bush, moving on relentlessly before they seem to need to. Few birds are so obvious in their daily movements. Although they remain together as a unit, long-tailed tit parties regularly join larger, mixed flocks of small birds, especially other species of tits.

VOICE
They call to each other with continual 'see-see-see' or 'see-see-see-see' notes, filling the air with their 'sees' and splutters.

IDENTIFICATION
Long-tailed tits have an unmistakable shape – nothing else comes close. They have red eyes, minute bills and rosy-pink colouring on shoulders, rump, flanks and belly. Adults have a black line that runs from above the eye in an arc to the mantle. Apart from this, the head is white. Juveniles have dusky sides to their faces, with only chin and crown white. They lack the pink coloration and the tails are shorter.

Long tails that flick

ADULT

Fly in parties

Rosy-pink colouring

Red eye

Minute bill

WHERE FOUND
Widespread resident in lowlands. Also woodland and scrub.

JUVENILE

FLIGHT
When crossing open ground, the long-tailed tit's flight is erratic, whirring, slightly undulating and not very fast; the tail sticks out behind, suddenly a nuisance.

ROOSTING

At night, groups huddle together for warmth. Most other birds don't do this, but long-tailed tits have tiny bodies that lose heat rapidly. Most group members are related.

Roosting together for warmth

GARDEN TIPS

Will come to bird-tables for suet, crumbs and oatmeal. Have recently taken to feeding from peanut feeders, but cannot take whole nuts. Prefer to nest in thorny shrubs, such as berberis and bramble.

NEST

Unlike other tits, which use holes, long-tailed tits build their intricate nests in the open, among branches. The basic, domed framework is of moss, bound with cobwebs. Lichens are used on the outside for camouflage. The interior is lined with up to 2000 feathers (collected from dead birds, roosts, etc). Entrances typically face south, to take advantage of the sun.

Domed nest made of moss, cobwebs and lichen

BREEDING

Some pairs get help when eggs hatch (usually from relatives of the male whose nests have failed).

Willow tit *Parus montanus*

A plain brown, black-capped tit which is less noisy and demonstrative than its relatives. It is notoriously similar to the marsh tit, and great care needs to be taken to tell them apart. Far and away the best method is voice: willow tits, when they call at all, give a buzzy, evenly stressed 'zur-zur-zur' and harsh 'tchay-tchay'. The marsh tit has a characteristic 'pit-chou' call, given in a sneezy burst, and sometimes elaborated into a phrase 'chicka-bay-bay-bay'. Willow tits are generally uncommon in gardens, but will visit from neighbouring suitable habitat: damp scrub or woodland (especially with alder and birch), coniferous woodland, and hedgerows. They tend to wander more than marsh tits, so are more likely to turn up in gardens unexpectedly.

IDENTIFICATION
In most willow tits, the tail is messier and distinctly notch-ended, in a 'W'. (In the marsh tit, it is squarer.) Some willow tits show subtle white edges to the end of the tail.

WHERE FOUND
Resident and widely but patchily distributed in England and Wales; not in Ireland and only in extreme south-west Scotland.

Dark, not glossy, cap

Tail ends in a 'W'

WILLOW TIT

Bull-necked and large-headed

Messy, notch-ended tail

Glossy cap

MARSH TIT

Squarer tail-end

Flanks cleaner

SIMILAR SPECIES
Gardens which have willow tits don't often have marsh tits and vice versa, so seeing them together is unlikely.

GARDEN TIPS

If your area has willow tits, strap a rotting birch stump, about 2 m (6½ ft) high and 20 cm (8 in) wide, to a garden tree. They may use this to excavate a nest. Although insect-eaters in summer, they will take nuts and seeds in winter.

NESTING

Willow tits, unlike marsh tits, excavate their own hole for the nest; they have strong muscles at the back of the neck, giving them their somewhat bull-necked appearance.

Will take peanuts in winter

Distinctive crest

CRESTED TIT

In central north Scotland, especially near conifer woods, look out for this unmistakable bird. It will come to nuts; sometimes to bird-tables. Will use nest-boxes, hole diameter 3–3.8 cm (1¼–1¾ in).

Marsh tit *Parus palustris*

This bird is NOT found in marshes, it's a woodland species. Another neat, plain brown, black-capped tit, the marsh is better proportioned, perkier and noisier than its relative the willow tit, but less effervescent than great or blue tits. It is more common in gardens than the willow tit; any gardens backing on to dry woodland with a good understorey stand a good chance of hosting it, especially if oak and beech trees are nearby. Once established, pairs never move far from their home; instead they remain in the same exclusive territory throughout the year. As a result, 'flocks' of marsh tits (or willow tits) seldom if ever occur (but look out for family parties in late summer). Within the confines of their territory, marsh tit pairs will join roaming tit parties.

WHERE FOUND
Resident throughout England and Wales, but not in Ireland; in Scotland it's creeping into the far south-east.

IDENTIFICATION
Note that the marsh tit has no wing-bars at all, and no white patch on the nape.

COAL TIT

GREAT TIT

MARSH TIT

No white patch on nape

No wing-bar

BLUE TIT

Feeding on beech mast

GROUND FEEDING
Marsh tits feed much more on the ground than willow tits. In some areas, they take large amounts of beech mast. Both marsh and willow tit tend to feed lower down than the more colourful species.

FOOD STORAGE

All the 'brown' tits store food, tucking it away, item by item, in small cracks such as bark fissures. It is estimated that some store over 100,000 items per year. Most food is retrieved the same day, although marsh tits have been shown to have a very good memory, and sometimes up to three days may elapse before collection.

GARDEN TIPS

Will feed on peanuts, fat and seeds. Not a great nest-box user but may use an enclosed box, sited low, with an entrance hole of 2.5–3.5 cm (1–1½ in) in diameter.

Storing food
in bark

VOICE

As well as their distinctive calls, marsh and willow tits have different songs. The marsh tit sings a repeated double-note like that of a great tit or coal tit, but faster and more rattling – 'pitchu-pitchu-pitchu', with the first note almost lost. The willow tit makes a sweeter sound – 'siu-siu-siu', less bubbly, almost sad.

NESTING

Quite unlike the willow tit, the marsh tit does not excavate its own nest-hole. Like most other tits, it uses existing natural holes. Occasionally, marsh tits take over holes already excavated by willow tits, causing identification problems.

Coal tit *Parus ater*

Usually coming third in the abundance list after the blue tit and great tit, the tiny, game coal tit makes a welcome change at the garden nut-feeder. It tends to be 'bullied' by these other species, so it patiently waits its turn at the feeder, quickly grabs a whole peanut, then hastens away, carrying its prize to a safe place to eat it or store it. Smallest of the typical, short-tailed tits, the coal tit shares its plain, brownish appearance with marsh and willow tits, but has a unique white stripe down the back of its neck, 'like a badger'. It also has two dotted white wing-bars.

VOICE
Song very similar to great tit, a repeated double note 'see-choo, see-choo, see-choo…', sweeter and less cheerful than larger species; often like sound of bicycle-pump. Calls varied,.

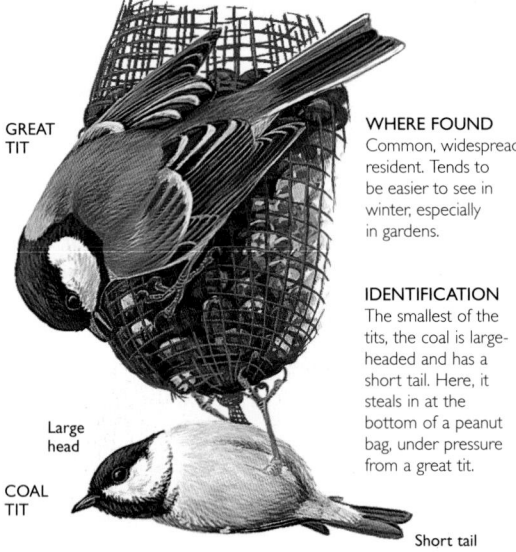

GREAT TIT

Large head

COAL TIT

Short tail

WHERE FOUND
Common, widespread resident. Tends to be easier to see in winter, especially in gardens.

IDENTIFICATION
The smallest of the tits, the coal is large-headed and has a short tail. Here, it steals in at the bottom of a peanut bag, under pressure from a great tit.

FOOD STORAGE
Like the other 'brown' tits, coal tits regularly store food, usually wedging seeds or peanuts into cracks in tree bark, less often among needles. In the autumn, they often forage on the ground for fallen seeds, some for consumption and some for storage.

White stripe down back of neck

YOUNG

Sexes look alike, but
young birds have a
yellowish wash to
them, especially on
the cheeks. Adult
birds in Ireland also
show this coloration.

**Yellowish wash
to cheeks**

NEST

Coal tits often nest very low down, in holes
in walls, tree roots and stumps. Coal tits have
large broods (like most tits) of between seven
and 11, which are fed on insects and spiders.
Coal tits will nest twice in good years.

**Coal tit with spider
prey for young**

FEEDING

The thin bill
(thinner than in
other tit species)
is an adaptation
for feeding among
conifer needles, this
bird's true home.

Thin bill

GARDEN TIPS

Coal tits like peanuts, fat and seeds. They benefit if there are several
feeders, to reduce the competition from other species. They eat
aphids in late summer and favour gardens with conifers, especially for
breeding. They will use nest-boxes with an entrance hole of 2.5–3.5
cm (1–1½ in) diameter (as blue tit). Try siting one low, or on a
conifer. Blue and great tits tend to occupy the best (higher) holes.

111

Blue tit *Parus caeruleus*

Unmistakable and hard to miss, the blue tit is an abundant, colourful, entertaining visitor to almost every garden. Despite its size, it is bold, noisy and pugnacious. Ever acrobatic, blue tits bring skills perfected in the treetops to bear in exploiting every kind of feeding opportunity, from peanut feeders and coconut bells to cream from milk-bottles. They can even be persuaded to take food directly from the hand. Although smaller than many other birds, blue tits are quite able to hold their own against aggressive competition from larger species; hence this is one of the most successful of all garden birds.

WHERE FOUND
Common throughout our area all year round. Prefers deciduous trees, especially in summer.

IDENTIFICATION
Small size, sky-blue crown and thin, dark stripe through eye distinguish it. Sexes are alike. Some individuals have a small, dark streak down belly – not to be confused with great tit's bold stripe.

Blue crown

Thin, dark stripe through eye

FLIGHT
A weak fluttering. On longer trips, undulates as with most small birds.

Commonly hangs upside-down on feeders

FORAGING
Perky and agile, blue tits are able to feed upside-down, sideways – in almost any contortion! Flocks wander, briefly visiting many gardens each day before moving on to the next: 200 different individuals may visit one garden in a day.

VOICE AND DISPLAY

When excited, individuals raise sky-blue crown feathers. Often perches in upright, alert posture, constantly flicking tail. Never silent, makes dynamic scolds of many syllables. Song is a crystal-clear trill with a few introductory notes, quite unlike that of other tits.

In spring, males have a special whirring display flight, like a butterfly or moth.

Raises crown feathers when excited

Whirring display flight

BREEDING

Timed to coincide with the maximum availability of summer food, especially caterpillars. Eggs laid in April. Broods are huge: 11 is average, 16 not unusual. The youngsters spill out in June and become a common sight in gardens. They have a yellowish wash, especially about the cheeks. Their chirping begging calls are one of the sounds of high summer.

Yellowish wash to cheeks of young

GARDEN TIPS

Blue tits readily come to almost any kind of feeder and will eat peanuts, seeds, fat, suet, meat bones and coconut. They also harvest many types of insect, including greenfly, and will eat some seeds, eg, nettle and berries, such as blackberries. They readily uses nest-boxes with an entrance hole of 2.5–3.5 cm (1–1½ in) diameter. Blue tits will exclude competing great tits from nest-holes.

Great tit *Parus major*

Being the largest of the tit family, the great tit's bulk makes it the dominant species at feeding stations, with a tendency to bully other birds away. It also gets the best tree-hole sites in which to nest – there's no democracy in the bird world. Occasionally this aggressive bird kills nestlings or adults of smaller species, but this is a rare event, and far more often it terrorizes the local caterpillar population! In behaviour, the great tit is typically perky like all the members of its family, moving briskly and breezily, but perhaps without the feverish restlessness of a blue tit or coal tit. It also spends more time feeding on the ground and on tree trunks.

IDENTIFICATION
A colourful species, strikingly turned out in yellow, blue, green and black. Both sexes have a bold black stripe down the yellow breast.

WHERE FOUND
Abundant: the second most common tit after blue tit. Occurs year-round throughout our area. Also woodland.

MALE

Slightly brighter-coloured

Wider breast-stripe, especially towards the belly

VOICE
From January to June the male gives a strong, cheerful performance, a repeated 'teacher, teacher, teacher' with an upbeat ring. It's a dominant sound in early spring woodland. There are constant variations, with each male having several versions. A very familiar call is a cheery 'pink pink', almost identical to a chaffinch.

Narrower black stripe

Male in song

FEMALE

YOUNG
From June onwards, young great tits appear. They are similar to the adults, but less brightly coloured; the black head markings are dusky, not shiny.

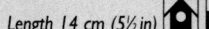 

GARDEN TIPS

Great tits feed on nuts (peanuts, hazelnuts), suet and other scraps. They are very enthusiastic nest-box users, more so than any other bird, and will use an enclosed nest-box, with an entrance hole of 29 mm (1¼ in) or more.

CATERPILLARS

In summer, adults and young feed on insects, especially caterpillars. A pair may capture 10,000 individual insects at this time, taken into the nest-hole one by one. This might seem to be a devastating exploitation of the caterpillar harvest, but it isn't: in fact a single large oak tree might hold 100,000 caterpillars.

YOUNG

Dusky head markings

Single white wing-bar

FLIGHT

Confident. Flies fast and straight in short bursts, more smoothly and undulating in longer trips – never looking as feeble as, eg, a flying blue tit. Shows a single wing-bar and white outer tail feathers (not on other tits, but beware nuthatch).

White outer tail feathers

GREAT TIT   NUTHATCH   CHAFFINCH

GROUND FEEDING

Great tits feed on the ground more regularly than most tits, often joining other birds above feeding with a nuthatch and a chaffinch on fallen beech mast.

Nuthatch *Sitta europaea*

The distinctive shape and markings are like an anaemic version of a kingfisher! But the nuthatch is a woodland bird, most often seen creeping up and down tree trunks and larger branches, keeping tight against them and progressing with a characteristic jerky action. Commonly it holds on upside-down, as if ready to dive off head-first. Its ability to move up, down and sideways on trunks distinguishes it from the treecreeper, which always creeps upwards, never downwards. The nuthatch is solidly built but not fat, and always looks immaculate. It can be a tetchy and aggressive visitor to bird-feeders.

VOICE
Its restless movements are accompanied by a variety of cheerful calls, especially 'chwit', easily imitated by a simple whistle.

FEEDING
Commonly wedges nuts into tree crevices and hammers at them for all it's worth – hence the name derivation 'nut-hack'. Hammering sounds heard in woodland could be this species, the great tit, marsh tit or any of the woodpeckers.

WHERE FOUND
Requires presence of large, mature deciduous trees. Only in southern half of Britain, and not in Ireland. Resident.

IDENTIFICATION
This head-down posture is very typical. Both sexes are a smart blue-grey above and sandy-brown below, with a striking black stripe through the eye. Male shows richer chestnut flanks, which sharply contrast with the buff belly. The female has duller flanks, grading into the belly colour.

MALE

Distinct black stripe through eye

Chestnut flanks

TERRITORY

Pairs remain together on territory all year, rarely wandering; so gardens without nuthatches are unlikely to acquire them suddenly. They will, however, join up with nomadic tit parties which pass through their boundaries.

Nuthatch with roving tit flock

FLIGHT

Strongly undulating, recalling a small woodpecker. When the bird lands, white spots at the end of the tail become visible.

NEST

Nests in tree-holes which, uniquely among British birds, is reduced in diameter by plastering with mud to a precise nuthatch-sized squeeze. This prevents competition with starlings. Will also use nest-boxes which, whatever their size, they will liberally coat with mud around the hole and in the cracks.

White spots to outer tail

FEMALE

Duller flanks grading into belly colour

GARDEN TIPS

Nuthatches will eat any nuts and also some seeds. Try wedging hazelnuts into tree bark and watch nuthatches hammering them open. They will use nest-boxes with an entrance hole to 3.5 cm (1¼ in) diameter. Try providing mud to help them cement their entrance hole. Unless your garden is adjacent to suitable habitat – mature, broad-leaved woodland – you are unlikely to attract them.

Treecreeper *Certhia familiaris*

This unique bird is most often seen creeping up tree trunks in short, jerky hops, looking mouse-like as its body is pressed close to the bark. A shy, quiet, retiring species, it is often difficult to detect because of the marvellous camouflage afforded by its brown mottled plumage. Treecreepers are birds of woodland, and they favour larger gardens with plenty of trees. They can be attracted by smearing suet or crushed nuts over fissures in tree bark, where the birds can find them in the normal course of their 'tree-creeping'. Only the nuthatch has a similar lifestyle of searching the surface of boughs and trunks, but it looks quite different and, unlike the treecreeper, can also move downwards and sideways.

VOICE
The call is a sibilant whistle repeated at regular intervals, like a rotated squeaky tap. The song is a quiet falling phrase which rises at the end.

WHERE FOUND
Common, widespread resident. Easily overlooked.

IDENTIFICATION
Long, curved bill for reaching insects hiding in nooks and crannies. Long, stiff tail for support when climbing trees. One theory suggests that the gleaming white breast reflects light into the secret places where insects lurk.

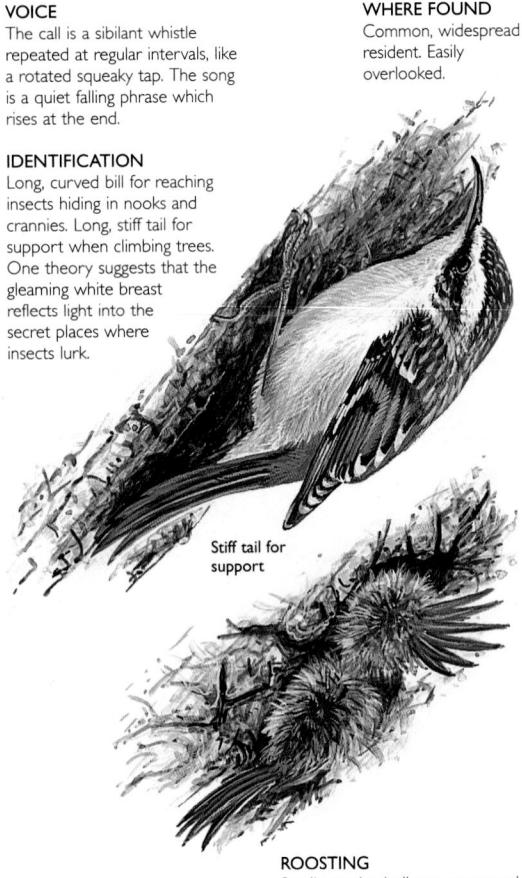

Stiff tail for support

ROOSTING
Small roosting hollows are carved in tree bark. The wellingtonia, with its very soft bark, is often used as a roost tree.

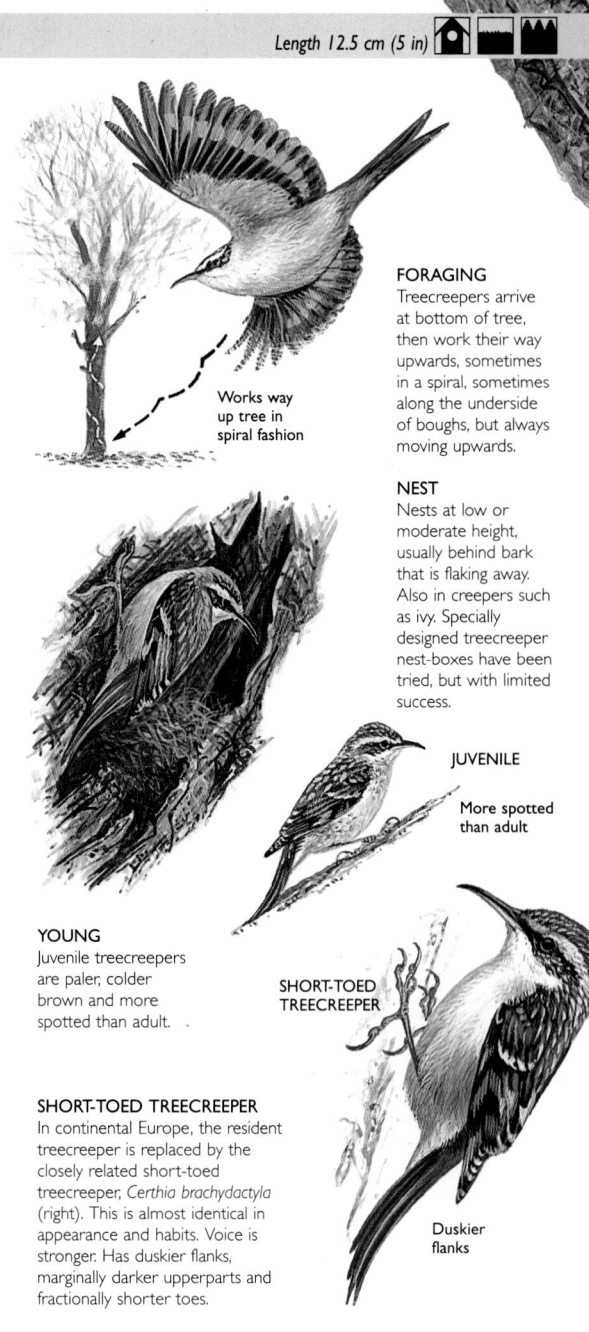

Works way up tree in spiral fashion

FORAGING
Treecreepers arrive at bottom of tree, then work their way upwards, sometimes in a spiral, sometimes along the underside of boughs, but always moving upwards.

NEST
Nests at low or moderate height, usually behind bark that is flaking away. Also in creepers such as ivy. Specially designed treecreeper nest-boxes have been tried, but with limited success.

JUVENILE
More spotted than adult

YOUNG
Juvenile treecreepers are paler, colder brown and more spotted than adult.

SHORT-TOED TREECREEPER

SHORT-TOED TREECREEPER
In continental Europe, the resident treecreeper is replaced by the closely related short-toed treecreeper, *Certhia brachydactyla* (right). This is almost identical in appearance and habits. Voice is stronger. Has duskier flanks, marginally darker upperparts and fractionally shorter toes.

Duskier flanks

119

Jay *Garrulus glanurius*

The jay is an unmistakable bird, always exciting to see, no matter how familiar it becomes. It maintains an exotic, otherworldly air, both in its colourful plumage and in its cautious, wary treatment of humans. Although shy and diffident by nature, it has recently taken to visiting garden bird-tables. To be a regular, however, it needs the presence nearby of large, mature deciduous trees, especially oaks, which are its real home. In summer, jays seem almost to disappear, living most of their lives high in the leafy canopy, or down among the shady litter. In autumn, however, they spend a month or so harvesting the acorn crop, moving about in small parties, and generally become very conspicuous.

VOICE

Draws attention to itself by its very loud, harsh screeching, sounding discordant and angry. Its habit of shouting at the slightest danger has earned it the nickname 'guardian of the forest'.

IDENTIFICATION

Jays pose no problems at all of identification: spectacular birds, with a unique combination of pink, black, white and blue. Sexes are alike. On the ground and in trees, jays move in heavy, confident hops.

Spectacular plumage

WHERE FOUND
Widespread, common resident, but more scarce in Scotland and Ireland.

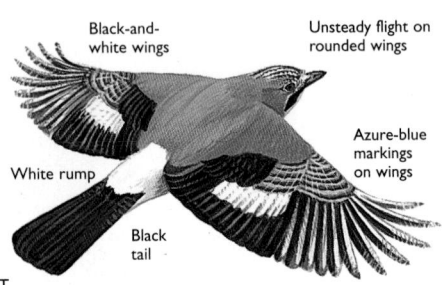

Black-and-white wings

Unsteady flight on rounded wings

Azure-blue markings on wings

White rump

Black tail

FLIGHT

Distinctive, rather fluttering and unsteady on rounded wings. As it flies, look for the bright white rump contrasting with the black tail – it's the largest woodland bird with a white rump.

ACORNS

In autumn, jays spend all the daylight hours collecting acorns, which they hide away in secret places for retrieval during the winter. Each bird may collect up to 5000 acorns in all, storing several at once, and apparently remembering where every one was left. Parties of commuting jays are a common sight in October and November, flying to and fro with their crops bulging with as many as nine acorns at a time.

Party of jays
gathering acorns

GARDEN TIPS

Jays feed on nuts, fruit and also eggs. They are shy, but can become regular visitors to gardens. They will often visit early in the morning. They will nest in trees and bushes.

NEST

The nest is built at moderate height in a tree or bush. It is very carefully concealed, and the adults are extremely cautious in their approaches to it. Three to seven eggs are laid, and the young are sometimes fed on the nestlings of smaller birds.

ANTING

In summer, watch for a curious behaviour known as 'anting', in which jays and other birds allow ants to crawl all over their plumage, and may even rub them along their flight feathers as if preening. The birds adopt an ecstatic posture, so whatever the function of anting – the removal of feather parasites has been suggested – the birds seem to enjoy it.

Jay allowing ants
to crawl over it

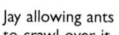

121

Magpie *Pica pica*

The magpie seems to inspire love and hatred in equal measure among garden-watchers. While it endears itself by its perkiness and cheek – swaggering across the lawn, raising its long tail, chattering frequently and challengingly – it makes itself unpopular by its habit of attacking and eating smaller birds, young or old, apparently ravaging every nesting attempt of garden blackbirds and thrushes – and doing this in full view of householders. It's certainly a character, black-and-white in both colour and conduct. Like all members of the crow family, the magpie is intelligent, and this robbing of nests is merely taking advantage of nutritious, readily available food. The same intelligence enables it to exploit a wide range of feeding opportunities.

IDENTIFICATION
The tail of the magpie, black but with colourful iridescence when light shines on it, is important to its owner. Males have longer tails than females, and the length of any bird's tail is an indication of its status within the social system. Youngsters, naturally, have the shortest tails!

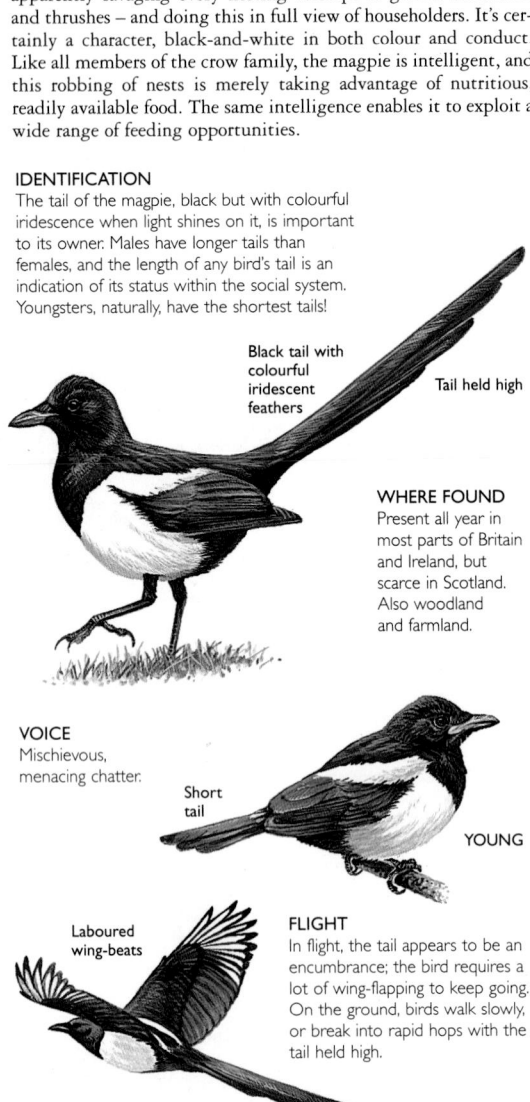

Black tail with colourful iridescent feathers

Tail held high

WHERE FOUND
Present all year in most parts of Britain and Ireland, but scarce in Scotland. Also woodland and farmland.

VOICE
Mischievous, menacing chatter.

Short tail

YOUNG

Laboured wing-beats

FLIGHT
In flight, the tail appears to be an encumbrance; the bird requires a lot of wing-flapping to keep going. On the ground, birds walk slowly, or break into rapid hops with the tail held high.

NEST

The nest, made of sticks and mud, is almost as distinctive as the bird, and is a common sight in suburban areas when the leaves have fallen. Most nests are low-down, at least in comparison with crows' nests, and are domed, not cup-shaped. They take three weeks to build from scratch. The roof of the dome is an adaptation to prevent nest-predation by crows. Additionally, the nest is often built in – and from – thorny vegetation. One enterprising pair made their nest out of wire.

Nest deep in
thorny vegetation

Magpie taking
young bird
from nest

THE VILLAIN

This sight of magpies taking young birds is such a common one in gardens that it upsets many people. In fact, the total amount of damage caused by magpies is probably less severe than appearances suggest. Many species of garden bird are almost entirely unaffected. The main victims are blackbirds, thrushes and chaffinches.

GARDEN TIPS

Takes scraps from the ground and the bird-table. Perhaps magpies are to be discouraged, as they take young birds of other species. There is no easy cure for magpie attacks. Uses thorn trees and hedgerows for nesting.

Bowing and tail-
wagging display

DISPLAY

Magpies display with much tail-wagging, bowing and wing-flapping – and with lots of noise. Birds don't breed until they are nearly two years old, then they settle with the same partner for life.

123

Jackdaw *Corvus monedula*

This is the smallest of the black crows, and the only one with a pale eye and extensive grey plumage around the head. It moves jauntily, with quicker movements than its relatives, and without their menace. Even so, it is bold and inquisitive, always ready to take advantage of feeding opportunities – and this can include regular visits to the bird-table. In many suburban and rural settings, jackdaws are a familiar sight on rooftops, where they use chimney-pots for their nests and forage in nearby streets and gardens. The jackdaw is an intelligent bird, with a well-deserved reputation for stealing bright-looking objects out of sheer curiosity: if you're in a 'jackdaw area', don't leave valuables around in the garden.

WHERE FOUND
Present all year, and widely distributed. Also cliffs.

VOICE
Cheerful 'chack' and variations, hence its name.

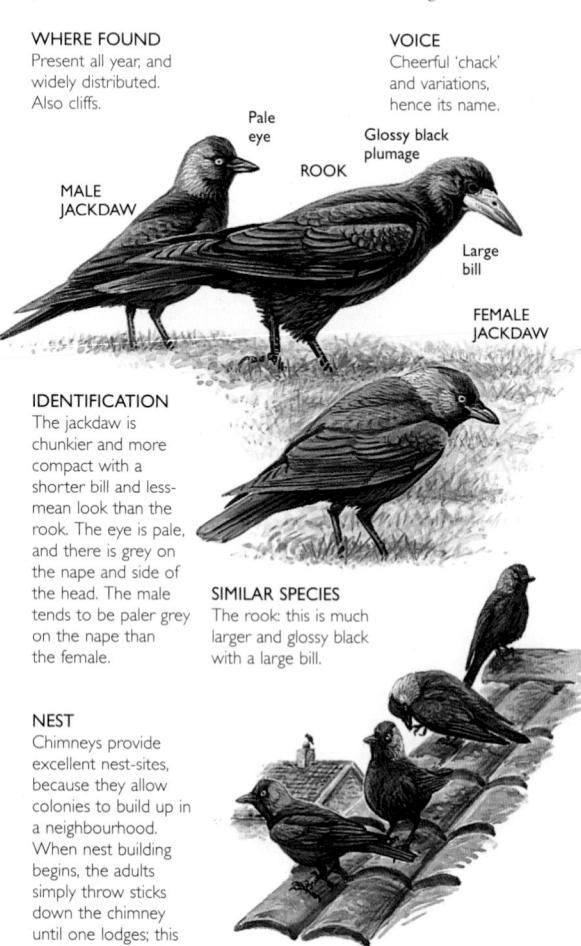

Pale eye

Glossy black plumage

ROOK

MALE JACKDAW

Large bill

FEMALE JACKDAW

IDENTIFICATION
The jackdaw is chunkier and more compact with a shorter bill and less-mean look than the rook. The eye is pale, and there is grey on the nape and side of the head. The male tends to be paler grey on the nape than the female.

SIMILAR SPECIES
The rook: this is much larger and glossy black with a large bill.

NEST
Chimneys provide excellent nest-sites, because they allow colonies to build up in a neighbourhood. When nest building begins, the adults simply throw sticks down the chimney until one lodges; this can become a serious fire hazard.

124

YOUNG

Most young emerge from the nest in June – breeding is timed to coincide with good numbers of insects on the grassy fields where jackdaws feed. They lack the grey feathering around the head and have brownish, eyes.

Lacks grey
feathering
on head

YOUNG

Brown,
not pale,
eyes

Blunt-
ended
wings

Fast flight

GARDEN TIPS

Jackdaws eat scraps and nest in chimneys (block these off if they are unwelcome), ruins and tree-holes. They usually use large enclosed boxes which have a 15 cm (6 in) entrance hole to them.

Evening
aerobatics

AEROBATICS

In the evening, colony members often indulge in impressive mass aerobatics high in the air, circling and cartwheeling to a background of excited 'chack' calls. This happens above the colony, or, perhaps, above a winter roost. Watch to see how pairs keep together, even among the melée of birds.

FLIGHT

The jackdaw's flight is quite unlike that of the larger crows. It is much faster and more flapping (closer to flight of a pigeon). The wings don't have the 'fingered' effect seen on rooks and carrion crows, appearing instead somewhat blunt-ended.

125

Rook *Corvus frugilegus*

As a rule, rooks are more sociable than crows, but it's incorrect to say, as it often is, that crows are never seen in flocks – they are (especially at roost). The difference is in their breeding behaviour: rooks nest in colonies, crows' nests are spaced far apart. The rook is a more rural bird than the crow, flourishing in agricultural areas where its two basic requirements – tall trees for nesting and open ground for feeding – exist. Generally, it doesn't take to gardens easily: most visits are in the early morning, and it's a rather sparing user of bird-tables. Much of its time is spent on the ground in fields, taking leatherjackets, earthworms and vegetable matter.

IDENTIFICATION

Much the same size as the crow, to which it is closely related, the rook is distinguished by the pale grey patch of bare skin at the base of the bill. This bare patch makes the bill seem longer. It has a much more peaked forehead. Plumage is glossy bluish- or purple-tinged. It seems to wear 'baggy shorts' due to the loose feathering on the thighs.

SIMILAR SPECIES

The carrion crow has a heavy black bill and flatter forehead. Not such glossy plumage and no loose plumage on thighs. More often seen in towns and cities than rook.

Pale bill
at base

Glossy
plumage

ROOK

'Baggy-
shorts'
look

Heavy,
black bill

CROW

Matt-black
plumage

WHERE FOUND

A common bird, present virtually all year throughout Britain and Ireland. Mostly in countryside.

Freer, faster flight
than crow

FLIGHT

Typically, many rooks are seen together, commuting between feeding grounds and the nesting colony. The flight is slightly faster and freer than the crow's. Notice how these birds' crops bulge with the food they are carrying.

ROOKERIES

Colonies of rooks are termed 'rookeries', appropriately enough. Most are situated in tall trees, or sometimes in woods which have been continuously occupied for many hundreds of years. Many villages have their 'own' rookery. Jackdaws often share the same site, using holes in the same trees, or even the bases of rooks' nests. Watch for the many comings and goings, squabbles, triumphs and disasters.

VOICE

Among the rookery cacophony, listen for the basic 'caw' of the rook. It's a flatter, more even sound than the carrion crow's more angry effort, but the difference is subtle.

NEST

The rookery is occupied from the very early days of the year, a sign of the approach of spring. Eggs are often laid in March, once minor or major refurbishments to the nests are completed.

YOUNG

Rooks just out of the nest lack the white skin near the bill and are exceedingly similar to crows. Slightly more peaked forehead; more pointed bill.

YOUNG

Peaked
forehead

ROOK

GARDEN TIPS

Rooks will visit bird-tables to feed on scraps, such as fruit and carcasses. They nest in 'rookeries' in tall trees.

CROW

This, the typical crow, is a large, angry, cheerless bird, sinister to the core. It fails to win very much affection among garden-watchers. Usually encountered singly or in pairs, it also forms small non-breeding groups and larger roosting aggregations. The carrion crow is found in most gardens, and has no problem in living with people, but it remains wary and wild. It will use bird-tables and ground stations, attracted by a variety of scraps, and is drawn to rubbish tips, roadsides and other urban attractions. Its life is more suited to cities than its relative the rook, which needs agricultural land. Crows have a slow, ponderous walk and an equally slow, heavily flapping flight.

CARRION AND HOODED CROW
Although they look different, these are two forms of the same species. In areas where both races occur, they will interbreed.

WHERE FOUND
A very widespread bird, common almost everywhere; 'hooded' form in Scotland and Ireland.

Jet-black all over

CARRION CROW

Grey on back and underparts

HOODED CROW

VOICE
A carrion crow belts out its 'song' from the treetops in a suburban street. The head is lowered with each 'caw', the tail is fanned and the neck feathers are ruffled.

FEEDING

Crows have a varied diet, including many other birds, young or adults. They're often first on the scene to kill an ailing individual, or a helpless nestling that has fallen to the ground. In the Middle Ages, they were not averse to human flesh, fresh from the gallows or from the ravages of plague. Not surprisingly, many unflattering legends built up around them, generally associating them with bad luck. Watch out for crows dropping items from a height on to the ground. This is to break open difficult food items such as shellfish or snails.

Dropping shellfish to break it open

GARDEN TIPS

Carrion crows are difficult to keep out of gardens. They will come to bird-tables to take scraps and carcasses and will often feed on the ground. They are shy and wary. They need mature trees for nesting high up.

NEST

The 'crow's nest' is built high up, usually in a tall tree. Nests are in a territory that is occupied all year, round, providing food and shelter for both adults and young, and birds rarely venture outside it.

Crows are patient, conscientious parents

BREEDING

Four or five young are raised. They take three weeks to hatch, five weeks to leave the nest, and a further four or five weeks to become independent.

Starling *Sturnus vulgaris*

Starlings love gardens: lawns are perfect for them, and bird-tables even better. Gangs often visit and take over a bird-table like pirates overwhelming a galleon, scattering all the smaller birds and denying them any leftovers. This very well-known and lively bird is a real bustling character, always on the move, progressing with a jaunty, swaggering walk and an over-fast flying action. Distinctly greedy when feeding, it guzzles food down quickly, enough to give even the casual watcher indigestion! The sociable starling is always seen in groups – or flocks, or multitudes.

WHERE FOUND

The starling is found almost throughout Britain and Ireland. Because of many immigrants arriving here from the Continent, it's probably our most numerous bird in the winter.

IDENTIFICATION

Identified by its unusual shape with a pointed bill, short square tail and plump body. Plumages are complicated. In winter, adults are spotted all over the plumage, like snow. The female has slightly larger spots. In spring and summer, the spots disappear and the bill is yellow. Males have a blue bill base; females have a pink one.

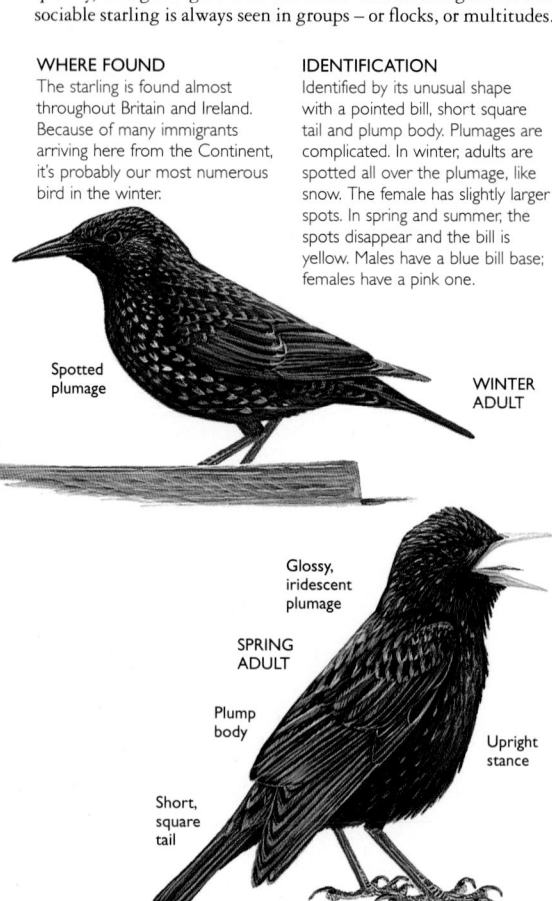

Spotted plumage

WINTER ADULT

Glossy, iridescent plumage

SPRING ADULT

Plump body

Upright stance

Short, square tail

VOICE

The starling's rambling song is a fast medley of whistles, chatters and clicks, quite unlike any other bird. It also contains many imitations, gleaned from its local environment. When singing, the male often points his bill to the sky, ruffles his neck feathers and quivers half-open wings.

NEST
Placed in a hole in a garden tree, or under the eaves of a building. Starlings also use enclosed nest-boxes. Up to six distinctively blue eggs are laid. This female is removing a faecal sac.

YOUNG
A group of adults and young feeds on a lawn in mid-summer. When the young hatch, they look utterly different from the parents – light brown all over – more like a separate species.

Light brown young birds

GARDEN TIPS
Feeds on scraps and carcasses. Probes for earthworms and leatherjackets. Uses eaves, tree-holes for nesting; will use an enclosed nest-box with a hole 5 cm (2 in) in diameter.

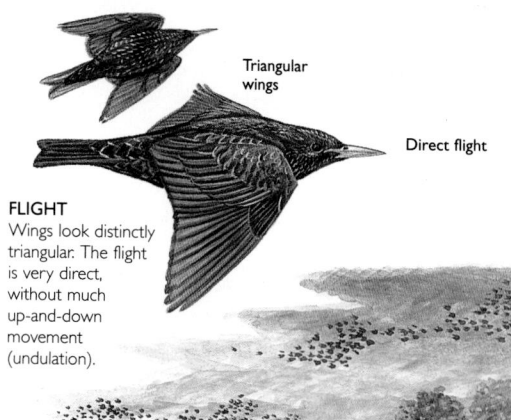

Triangular wings

Direct flight

FLIGHT
Wings look distinctly triangular. The flight is very direct, without much up-and-down movement (undulation).

ROOST
Starlings roost in huge numbers, sometimes tens of thousands. They use low bushes, and also buildings in city centres. Watching them as they wheel acrobatically over the roost, screeching deafeningly, is an unforgettable experience.

House sparrow *Passer domesticus*

Many people whose gardens are overrun with sparrows might be tempted to think that this is our commonest bird. In fact, it isn't, but its life and fortunes are so wrapped up in those of humans – depending on us for food, shelter and a nest-site – that it is most abundant where we are – in cities, towns, villages and farms. Just about every garden has sparrows, and almost everyone is familiar with their cheerful demeanour and bold intelligence. They always do things socially: they nest in loose colonies, roost in streetside shrubs, and feed or loaf around together.

VOICE
A variety of familiar cheeps and chirps.

WHERE FOUND
Common all year throughout Britain and Ireland, but avoids hills and mountains.

Grey crown and bill

Pale eyebrow

MALE

Black throat

IDENTIFICATION
In spring and summer, the male has a smart black throat and breast, grey crown, colourful wing pattern and slate-grey bill. The female lacks the bold patterning. Note the pale bill and obvious pale eyebrow.

Pale eye-brows

FEMALE

YOUNG

Yellow at bill base

YOUNG
The young are similar to females, but with yellow around the bill base, overflowing from the gape.

NEST

Very ragged, a product of 'cowboy builders'.
It is woven from grass stems into a roughly
domed shape, or is otherwise fitted into some
kind of hole, usually in a building. In some
areas, the insides of street-lights are used –
ideal for keeping the chicks warm at night.

COMFORT BEHAVIOUR

A group of sparrows dust-bathing
and preening. This is a favourite
pastime, especially in summer,
and probably serves to remove
parasites from the feathers.

Dust-bathing

FLIGHT

Confusing in flight,
sparrows can fly
straight along,
or undulate
like finches.
Care needs to
be taken when
identifying them.

FEEDING

Sparrows eat almost
anything; many urban
individuals seem to
subsist entirely on
bread. Peanuts are a
much more nutritious
alternative.

WINTER
MALE

GARDEN TIPS

If you have too many sparrows
monopolizing your bird-table,
try providing a number of
other feeding stations; or you
can put a sparrow-proof mesh
around the feeder to allow
only the smaller birds in.
Provide hay for nesting if
none is available.

WINTER MALE

Less smart. Dingier
cap. Smaller amount
of black on chin and
breast. Dull corn-
coloured bill.

Tree sparrow *Passer montanus*

The tree sparrow is a birdwatcher's bird – subtly different from the house sparrow, much less common, and something of an enigma. Gardens with this species are privileged, for tree sparrows are very fussy about where they live, and have a habit of disappearing from occupied sites almost overnight. The population fluctuates vastly over long cycles of years, for reasons that remain obscure. To add to its curiosity value, while the male and female house sparrow look quite different, the sexes in the tree sparrow are alike – there is no separate female plumage. This is probably to ensure that the two species remain isolated from one another and don't interbreed too often.

IDENTIFICATION

Obviously a sparrow, but is clearly different from the house sparrow. Tree sparrows have chocolate-brown caps, smart white collars, black spots on clean white cheeks and black-and-yellow bills. A slighter, neater, less effervescent bird than the house sparrow. Easy to overlook.

FEMALE HOUSE SPARROW

TREE SPARROW

MALE HOUSE SPARROW

FLIGHT

Flight patterns are similar. Listen for a distinctive, hard 'tek' call, not given by flying house sparrow.

MALE HOUSE SPARROW

TREE SPARROW

One white wing-bar

Two white wing-bars

WHERE FOUND

Most tree sparrows live near agricultural land in the lowlands of Britain and Ireland, and there seems to be a bias to the east of both countries. Present all year where it occurs.

Chocolate-brown cap

Black spot on clean white cheek

Male displaying outside nest-box

DISPLAY

Tree sparrows will use nest-boxes. A male displays by lowering head and ruffling head feathers. If a female arrives, he will fly towards the nest-hole and farther afield in a fluttering display flight. After a while, he enters the box and brings out some nest material. This understated performance leads to the pair-bond being formed.

NEST

Two or three broods of four to six young can be raised in a season, in a nest as scruffy as the house sparrow's. It is fairly stuffed into the box, or into a hole in a tree or wall. In general, tree sparrows prefer to nest in small colonies.

GARDEN TIPS

Tree sparrows nervously visit bird-tables to eat seeds. They will use an enclosed nest-box, with an entrance hole 3 cm (1¼ in) in diameter (larger holes let in house sparrows). Is vulnerable to disturbance.

Yellow at bill base

YOUNG TREE SPARROW

YOUNG HOUSE SPARROW

YOUNG

Similar to the adults, if less boldly patterned. Like house sparrow fledglings, they have yellow at the bill base, but are otherwise quite different from the anaemic-looking youngsters of their relatives.

135

Chaffinch *Fringilla coelebs*

The chaffinch is consistently among the top ten most common garden birds in Britain. It's a cheerful, sociable character, which in winter is usually seen in flocks, either at the bird-table or, perhaps more typically, at ground stations. Flocks are sometimes dominated by one sex (*coelebs* is Latin for bachelor). In summer the chaffinch's character changes. It forsakes its flock instincts to defend a territory, and changes its diet from seeds to insects, so that all its needs, and those of its young, can be provided for on its doorstep. It's then that its familiar rattling song seems to echo from every wood, hedgerow and bushy garden in the land.

IDENTIFICATION
Recognized by its white shoulders and distinctive elongated shape, looking longer tailed than other finches or sparrows. Peaked head and seed-eater's thick bill. Broad white wing-bar and obvious white outer tail feathers. Male slightly larger than female with a more peaked head, especially in summer.

Broad white wing-bar

White shoulders

Long tail

WINTER MALE

Thick bill

WINTER PLUMAGE
In winter, male has blue-grey wash on the crown and nape, which intensifies in colour in spring (the dull feather edges are worn away to give a brighter undercoat).

FEMALE

FEMALE
Females have soft brown on head, breast and back.

Soft brown colour

WHERE FOUND
Common, widespread resident, with many thousands of extra continental birds visiting for the winter.

White outer tail feathers

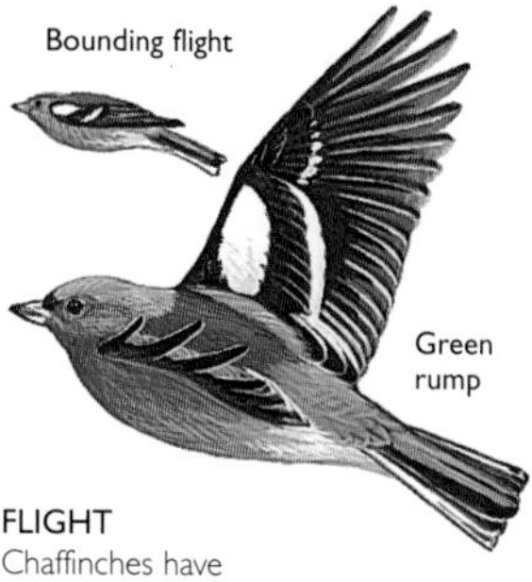

Bounding flight

Green rump

GARDEN TIPS

Chaffinches come to bird-tables, ground stations and hanging seed holders. They feed on sunflower and other seeds and many other scraps, but are not good at hanging on to peanut bags. They will nest in shrubs or small trees.

Peaked crown

FLIGHT

Chaffinches have strongly undulating flight, closing the wings every few beats. Look out for white outer tail feathers on long tail, and green rump.

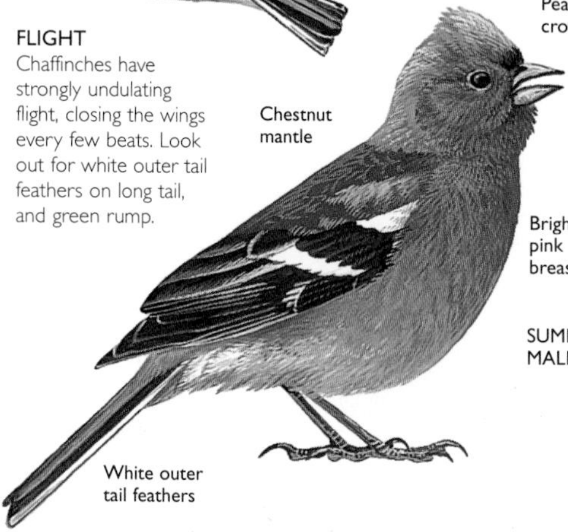

Chestnut mantle

Bright pink breast

SUMMER MALE

White outer tail feathers

VOICE

Male sings from February to July, performing with full vigour from an open perch. Each phrase, repeated regularly, is an accelerating rattle finishing with a flourish; it has been likened to the footsteps of a slow bowler in cricket approaching the crease and delivering the ball. The call is a loud, cheery 'Pink-pink'.

MALE CHAFFINCH

BRAMBLING

FEMALE CHAFFINCH

FEEDING

Hops or shuffles on ground. Beech mast is an important food source, shared by the closely related brambling. Note the white shoulders of the chaffinch and the orange shoulders of the brambling.

137

Brambling *Fringilla montifringilla*

An exciting winter visitor to more fortunate gardens, the brambling is the northern equivalent of the chaffinch. Our visitors come from Scandinavia or occasionally Russia, arriving in October and leaving in early spring. Their mission in Britain is to find and exploit beech nuts, their staple diet in winter, so not surprisingly areas with plenty of beech trees are most likely to attract them. But as winter moves on and the beechmast supplies run out, some bramblings come to gardens for seeds and peanuts instead. Despite the name, they have very little to do with brambles.

IDENTIFICATION

Look for the distinct orangey wash about the shoulders, upper breast and wing-bar; and for the black mottling on the back. Bramblings show white rumps and a short, deeply forked tail. Winter males have dark mottling on head and back, and more obvious spots on the flanks. Winter females are greyer on the head and have fewer flank flecks.

SIMILAR SPECIES

Male brambling often has a yellower bill than chaffinch, with a black tip. The bill itself is slightly bigger, with sharp edges, making it more efficient for opening up beechmast than the bill of the more generalist chaffinch. The two species look similar in shape and size, but the brambling is less common.

Dark mottling on head and back

WINTER MALE

Greyer on head

WINTER FEMALE

Mixed finch flock in winter

CAMOUFLAGE

Their attractive, subtle shades of colour act as camouflage when they feed among the fallen leaves of autumn and winter.

WHERE FOUND

Widespread in Britain, scarce in Ireland; the numbers in any one year depend on the supply of beech mast both here and on the continent.

FLIGHT

A mixed flock of finches takes off, and the distinction between chaffinch and brambling becomes much clearer. Note the white shoulders of the chaffinch and the white rump and orange shoulders of the brambling.

Black head and back

SPRING PLUMAGE

By early spring, the male is changing colour as its feathers wear, replacing the unremarkable mottling on head and back with a very smart pitch-black. It becomes a very handsome bird indeed.

SPRING MALE

Rich orange breast

GARDEN TIPS

As winter progresses, bramblings become more common in gardens, taking seeds and nuts from ground stations, and even settling on hanging peanut feeders. Watch from February onwards, unless your garden backs on to a beech wood.

139

Bullfinch *Pyrrhula pyrrhula*

In contrast to most finches, the bullfinch is a quiet bird, less perky in its movements than a chaffinch or a goldfinch, for instance. But it does have the bright plumage typical of a finch: the male has a bright, strawberry-coloured breast, and the female is plum-coloured. Such references to fruit are appropriate, for the bullfinch has earned itself a bad reputation for destroying the buds of cherries, gooseberries, pears and plums, in orchards and gardens. A single bird can remove buds at a rate of 30 per minute, giving a new slant to the term 'pick your own'. Most damage is done in the winter and early spring, and especially when the bullfinch's favourite natural food, ash mast, is in short supply. Many still welcome these birds, however, for their sheer beauty and novelty.

IDENTIFICATION
Rarely a problem to identify, the bullfinch has an exotic look, with colourful, silky plumage. The shape is top-heavy, with the bull-neck and large bill being offset by the broad black crown, which descends below the eye.

MALE

Grey back

Bull-necked appearance

Crimson breast

FEMALE

Plum-coloured breast

Heavy bill

Brown back

WHERE FOUND
Widely distributed resident throughout Britain and Ireland; less common in the north.

Single white wing-bar

Undulating flight

White rump

FLIGHT
A shy bird, the bullfinch prefers to stay hidden, feeding in thick cover. If discovered it flies hastily away. The flight is heavily undulating, like most finches. A very obvious white rump shows in flight, as does a single white wing-bar.

Feeding on
nettle and dock

GARDEN TIPS
Bullfinches rarely visit bird-tables but they will attack fruit and other buds. Birds can be discouraged by netting. They like ash mast and many weed seeds, eg, nettle and bramble. They prefer thick bushes and creepers for nesting.

VOICE
Bullfinches keep together by calling, making a very distinctive note – a soft, rather melancholy 'piu' that can be imitated by a whistle. In spring, males utter a very weak but curious medley of whistles and creaks, sounding like a pub sign swinging in the wind!

BREEDING
When young hatch, they are fed on seeds mixed with insects. Food collected by parents is stored in a special pouch in the floor of the mouth, which develops just for the breeding season.

NEST
They nest in a thick shrub, quite frequently in gardens, where several clutches of four to six eggs are raised.

YOUNG
When they leave the nest, the young lack the black crown of the adults and can look rather chaffinch-like. But they still have the top-heavy look, a white rump and a completely black tail.

No black crown

YOUNG

Black tail

FEEDING
Apart from fruit buds, bullfinches eat ash mast and a variety of other vegetable foods. Big flocks of bullfinches are rare.

Serin *Serinus serinus*

The serin is not a British bird, but is included here because it's a familiar garden user on the Continent, from France eastwards to Germany and Poland, and southwards to the Mediterranean. It has made several attempts to colonize Britain in recent times, but has not yet been successful; it appears that our wet and chilly climate is the main problem. A tiny, dynamic finch, the serin is recognizable by its exceptionally short, stubby bill and short, forked tail. Like all finches it eats seeds, which are usually collected on the ground, the birds foraging in small groups of 5–10 individuals. The serin is superficially similar to a number of other species, so be on your guard for it.

WHERE FOUND
Serins favour places with plenty of conifers, as these make the best trees for nesting.

VOICE
Characteristically noisy, uttering a 'tirrilit' flight call and other fast and breathless sounds.

IDENTIFICATION
The male serin is tiny and streaky yellow-green in colour. It is bright yellow about the head and breast, with a bright yellow rump. The female has an indistinct wing-bar. Serins have very small bills.

MALE

Brighter yellow than female

Indistinct wing-bar

SONG AND DISPLAY
In spring, males make themselves conspicuous by song and by display flight. The song is an intense, very fast jangle, a little bit like someone shaking a set of keys very quickly (also sounds like glass being ground). On occasions, singing birds lift themselves into the air and describe wide arcs and circles with slow, deliberate wing-beats and glides. (Greenfinches also do this, but have a quite different song.)

Circular display flight

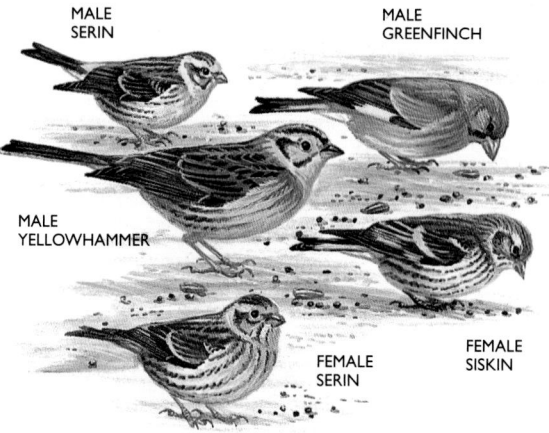

MALE
SERIN

MALE
GREENFINCH

MALE
YELLOWHAMMER

FEMALE
SERIN

FEMALE
SISKIN

SIMILAR SPECIES

Siskins are larger-billed than serins with obvious yellow wing-bars and yellow-green rumps. Yellowhammers are larger with longer tails and chestnut rumps. Greenfinches are largest and have huge bills. They have big yellow wing-bars and .green rumps.

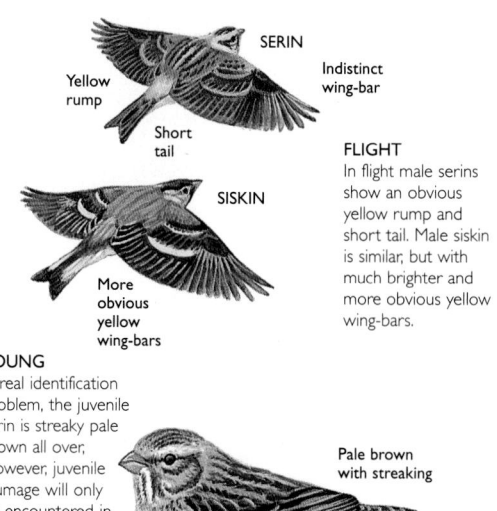

SERIN

Yellow
rump

Indistinct
wing-bar

Short
tail

SISKIN

More
obvious
yellow
wing-bars

FLIGHT

In flight male serins show an obvious yellow rump and short tail. Male siskin is similar, but with much brighter and more obvious yellow wing-bars.

YOUNG

A real identification problem, the juvenile serin is streaky pale brown all over; However, juvenile plumage will only be encountered in late summer; in September the youngsters of the year moult into adult plumage.

Pale brown
with streaking

JUVENILE

143

Greenfinch *Carduelis chloris*

Give the sparrows on your feeder a second look, and you'll probably find a greenfinch or two hiding among them. Similar in size and shape to the sparrow, the greenfinch can look fairly dull in the poor light of a winter's day, and is easily overlooked. However, it's a common bird in gardens, often gathering in large enthusiastic groups around peanut feeders, where its passion for these nuts knows no bounds – for some individuals, they form 97% of the winter diet! Ironically, the greenfinch is a 'generalist' for the rest of the year, harvesting more species of plant seeds than any other garden bird.

SIMILAR SPECIES
House sparrows look similar to greenfinches but show no yellow in the plumage. Male sparrows also have black chins. Sparrows have thinner bills and less forked tails.

SEED-EATERS
Greenfinches eat many kinds of seeds. They can deal with tiny nettle, dock or dandelion seeds as well as larger seeds that need crushing, such as sunflowers (greenfinches are a pest in sunflower fields).

Greenfinches and house sparrows on peanut feeder

Apple-green colour

Poisonous seed-coats must be removed

Bright yellow wing-bars

WHERE FOUND
A very common species in lowlands throughout Britain and Ireland. Resident.

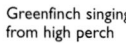

Greenfinch singing from high perch

VOICE AND DISPLAY

Males utter a drawn-out wheeze – 'greeeeen' – as part of a song based on fast and slow trills. They often embellish their performance with a fluttering, circular song flight, giving them an unusual elegance.

SUMMER MALE

Circular song flight

Forked tail

IDENTIFICATION

Plump, thickset finch, with upright carriage and a slightly fierce expression. Aptly named, the greenfinch is apple-green all over, with yellow flashes on the wings and tail. Winter plumage males are drabber than in summer and often greyer around head.

Streaking on crown and back

FEMALE

Duller-coloured than male

Yellow sides to tail

JUVENILE HOUSE SPARROW

JUVENILE GREENFINCH

No yellow in plumage

Bill smaller, darker

Wing and tail-pattern as adult

No streaks on underparts

Brownish-green and streaked

YOUNG

Young are in juvenile plumage from June to September and are similar to juvenile house sparrows.

GARDEN TIPS

Greenfinches eat peanuts and seeds, eg, black sunflower seeds. To attract them, plant sunflowers, mezereon, etc. The birds nest in hedges or small conifers. Often a few pairs will nest together. The long breeding season runs from April to August.

Goldfinch *Carduelis carduelis*

This sparklingly colourful, cheery bird is mostly evident in our gardens in the summer months, when it likes to take advantage of the glut of seeds to be found in almost any herbaceous border or 'wild patch'. Thistles are the firm favourite, accounting for a third of the entire diet of some individuals, but goldfinches also take teazel, dandelion, ragwort, groundsel and sometimes lavender. Small groups spend long periods of time clinging to the seed-heads of these plants, feeding busily, sometimes flitting from one plant to the other with a burst of yellow wings.

WHERE FOUND
A common species found throughout Britain and Ireland. Scarce in Scotland. Many, but not all, depart southwards in winter.

IDENTIFICATION
Males and females look much alike, although the male has slightly more red on its face. The black, white and red head, fawn-brown body plumage, and almost violent yellow wing-bars are unique as a combination.

Goldfinches feeding on thistles

Fawn brown body

Black, white and red head

VOICE
Much of the time, goldfinches twitter to themselves. Their 'tinkling' notes, often rendered 'tickelit' sound, upbeat and merry.

Broad yellow wing-bar

Light, bouncy flight

White rump

FLIGHT
When flying from plant to plant, look for the white rump and broad yellow wing-bar. Goldfinches have a very light, bouncing flight.

LATE BROODS

Goldfinches make use of wet summers; these delay the opening of the thistle-heads until quite late in the season, when they become available to the year's youngsters. Many pairs are still breeding as late as August, which is exceptional among British birds.

Young
lack head
markings
of adult

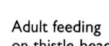

Adult feeding
on thistle heads

FEEDING

The small, whitish bill is narrower and more pointed than that of other finches, and is very useful for extracting the seeds of teazel. It does make the goldfinch a bit of a specialist, however, without the capability of opening larger seeds such as those of sunflowers.

GARDEN TIPS

Goldfinches will visit weedy patches with thistles, burdocks, dandelions and similar plants. Plant teazel and lavender to attract them. A rare visitor to bird-table or feeder. Nests in fruit trees and horse chestnuts.

NEST

Built in a tree or tall bush, often characteristically on the outermost twigs of a hanging bough, where it is extremely difficult to spot. Fruit trees and horse chestnuts are often chosen. The nest is a neat cup of moss, grass and small roots. Five or six eggs are laid in mid-May, when most resident birds already have young. The young are fed some insects in what is essentially a diet of seeds.

147

Siskin *Carduelis spinus*

This small finch of northern coniferous woods would be an unlikely candidate for any garden bird-list were it not for its passion for peanuts. Over the last 30 years, siskins have discovered peanut bags the length and breadth of the country, having been lured away from their more traditional winter feeding haunts among alders, birches and larches. A typical finch, the siskin is specially adapted to taking smaller seeds from among networks of slender branches, where it needs to be acrobatic to forage effectively. It's an easy step from here to hanging upside-down on a feeder, skilfully dodging pecks from greenfinches or sparrows.

IDENTIFICATION

The siskin is like a miniature greenfinch, but the yellow wing-bars go across, not along, the wings. The male has a coal-black crown and chin-patch. The female lacks black on the head and is more heavily streaked all over.

WHERE FOUND

A winter visitor to most of Britain. Local resident, mostly in the north, breeding in spruce or pine woods.

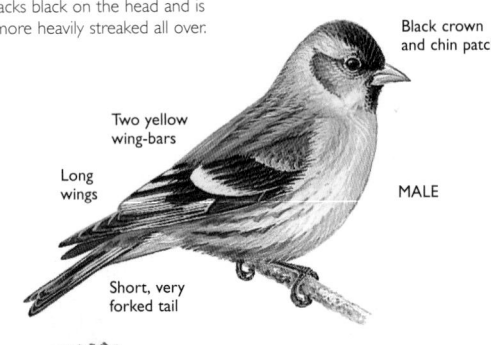

Black crown and chin patch

Two yellow wing-bars

Long wings

MALE

Short, very forked tail

Siskins at peanut feeder

FEMALE

MALE

FEEDING

Siskins seem to prefer red peanut-holders as opposed to any other colour, and it has been suggested that these bags resemble giant alder catkins, reminding the birds of their more normal foraging habits.

FLOCKS

If your garden has alders or birches, look for small flocks feeding silently among the branches. When disturbed, the flock suddenly cascades out in one or several tight groups, uttering a medley of creaky 'tseu' calls.

Siskin flock in birch tree

WINTER FEEDING

In late winter, siskins are often seen on the ground, feeding on seeds that have dropped from branches; or they might be down by a pool or pond, quenching their thirst.

DISPLAY

Watch out for the energetic flight display over conifers in spring, involving fluttering flight in loops and circles. The song, also given from a perch, is a twittering babble, including strange buzzes.

Double yellow wing-bar

Fluttering, looping display flight

GARDEN TIPS

Siskins feed on peanuts and other seeds, and sometimes on cypress early in the winter. Originally, siskins used to come to gardens only at the end of winter (February) when their supplies of wild seeds were diminishing, but now they will often visit much earlier in the season.

149

The redpoll is associated with birch and depends largely upon the seeds of this tree for its survival throughout the winter. Not surprisingly, therefore, gardens need birch if they are to attract redpolls. A few, however, may be drawn to stands of alder or other trees, including conifers. Small flocks feed acrobatically in the outermost branches, clinging to catkins, often upside-down. In silhouette they resemble tits until the obviously forked tail gives them away. Although redpolls visit most gardens only in winter, the species is resident, and may nest in some larger gardens with trees of medium height.

IDENTIFICATION
The 'red poll' refers to the forehead. All adults show this, as well as a black chin, yellow bill and some black in front of the eye. Females are more streaked on the breast than males.

WHERE FOUND
Widespread but never common or conspicuous.

VOICE
When disturbed or when moving some distance, they utter a distinctive flight call, a dry, rattling trill.

FEMALE

Black chin

Red forehead

Notched tail

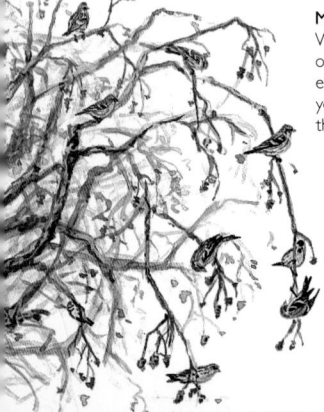

MIXED FLOCK
Winter flocks in birches or alders often contain siskins, blue tits or even goldfinches. Note the siskin's yellow wing-bars contrasting with the buffy wing-bars of the redpoll.

Length 11.5 cm (4¾ in)

MEALY REDPOLLS

A few continental redpolls visit us for the winter, mostly wintering in the east. These larger, paler birds are called 'mealy redpolls'.

MEALY REDPOLL

SPRING PINK

In spring, the reddish-pink colour on the male intensifies, making him a fine sight. At this time of year the birds become noisy: the dry, rattling call, intermixed with an additional metallic 'chee-chee-chee', constitutes the song, which is delivered in a dancing display flight.

SPRING MALE

Buffy wing-bar

Pink breast

Pink rump

GARDEN TIPS

To attract redpolls, plant birch or alder on which they will feed acrobatically among the catkins. Redpolls will visit bird-tables for scraps very infrequently, and they will not use peanut bags like their relative the siskin. They nest in low shrubs.

NEST

Most nests are placed low down or at moderate height in birches, willows or conifers, and sometimes apple trees. If possible, several pairs will nest in loosely scattered 'neighbourhood groups'. The young are fed mostly on seeds, with a few insects thrown in.

OTHER FOOD

At times redpolls will feed either on or close to the ground. They will eat seeds, such as thistle or burdock.

151

Yellowhammer _Emberiza citrinella_

Most people associate yellowhammers with long summer days, remembering how their dry 'little bit of bread and no cheese' song phrases carry across sun-drenched fields, accentuating the warmth and stillness. However, these attractive birds are just as much with us during the winter, and it's then that they take to feeding at garden stations where seeds and corn are provided. They prefer foraging on the ground rather than on the bird-table, and when they visit it is usually in groups of 10 or more. Being sociable, they flock and roost not only with their own kind, but also with finches and sparrows.

SONG
Male yellowhammers sing from the top of a fence post, on a wire or from a branch. The song rarely follows the sentence 'little bit of bread and no cheese' accurately – many singers omit the 'cheese'. The refrain may be repeated thousands of times a day, and long past mid-summer when most other birds have begun to wind down their performance.

IDENTIFICATION
Males have mainly a bright yellow head and a chestnut rump, and are streaked on the head, back and flanks. Females are duller and less streaked. Young birds are duller still with almost no yellow in the plumage. Birds of all ages have white outer tail feathers. Yellowhammers are identified from finches and sparrows by their slimline body and relatively long tail, a typical feature of buntings.

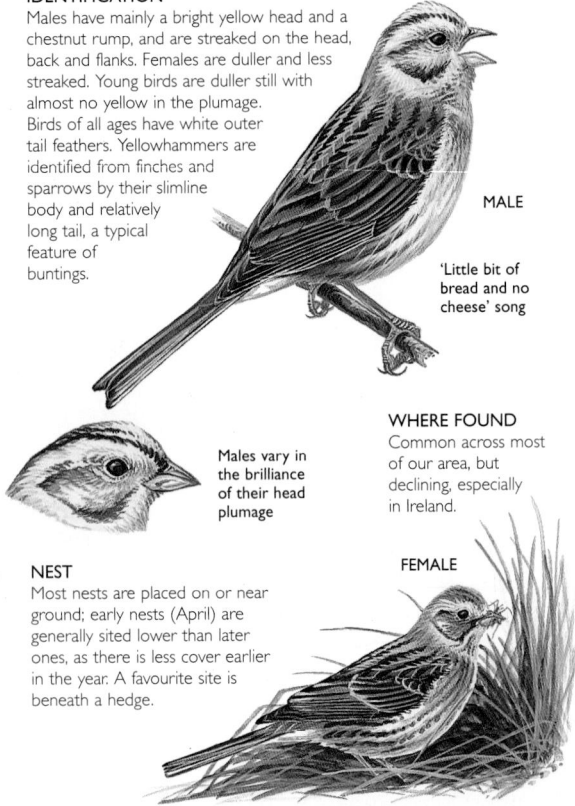

MALE

'Little bit of bread and no cheese' song

Males vary in the brilliance of their head plumage

WHERE FOUND
Common across most of our area, but declining, especially in Ireland.

FEMALE

NEST
Most nests are placed on or near ground; early nests (April) are generally sited lower than later ones, as there is less cover earlier in the year. A favourite site is beneath a hedge.

FLIGHT

Like other buntings, yellowhammers look very slim in flight, especially compared with the smaller finches, eg, the goldfinch. The flight goes up and down less steeply, too.

YELLOWHAMMER

Less undulating flight than finches

Chestnut rump and back

Tail notched

White outer tail feathers

GOLDFINCH

YOUNG

Two or three broods of three to five young are raised; they are drab and resemble sparrows, but have longer tails and lack a pale eyebrow.

YOUNG YELLOWHAMMER

Little yellow in plumage

Long tail

GARDEN TIPS

These birds will visit gardens to feed on corn and seeds. They also to eat fruit, including blackberries. Yellowhammers are most likely to be seen in gardens that back on to agricultural land, especially if there are plenty of hedgerows.

WINTER FLOCKS

In winter, yellowhammers flock with other birds, eg, ,sparrows, chaffinches and bramblings,.and visit feeding stations for corn and other seeds. Gardens near scrub or heathland are may be visited.

153

Reed bunting *Emberiza schoeniclus*

Most of us see reed buntings in our gardens only in late winter when the natural supply of seeds elsewhere is getting low. They are not common garden birds, and have only cottoned on to the idea of using artificial food supplies in the last 10 years or so. Originally birds of reedbeds and wet areas, reed buntings have made a significant shift towards inhabiting drier places in recent times, and the use of gardens is part of that revolution. Although winter is the best time to see them close to, in spring and summer the males are very smart, with a bold black head and white collar. Outside the breeding season, they can be mistaken for sparrows.

IDENTIFICATION
The reed bunting is distinguished by its long tail, white outer tail feathers and obvious white moustache. In winter, the male reed bunting's head looks a dull, messy black colour. In spring, this head pattern turns jet black and white, with a conspicuous white collar and moustache.

SIMILAR SPECIES
Compared to the reed bunting, the female house sparrow has a shorter tail with dark outer feathers and no moustache. The female yellowhammer has a yellowish wash and a chestnut rump. Yellowhammers lack an obvious moustache.

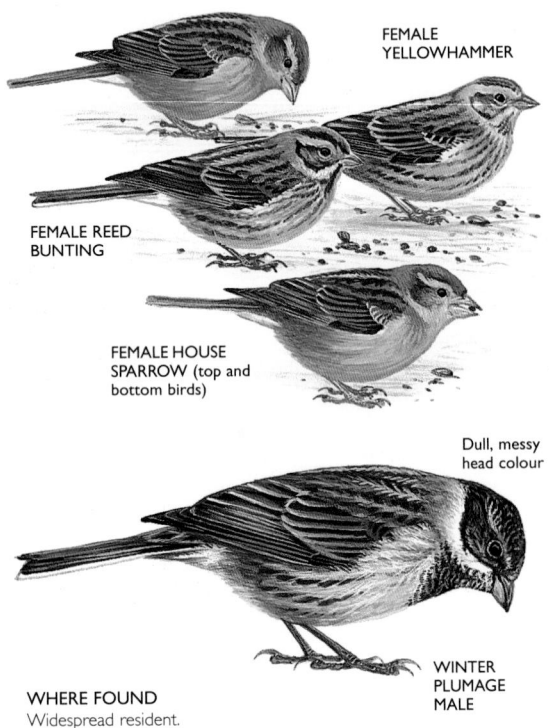

FEMALE YELLOWHAMMER

FEMALE REED BUNTING

FEMALE HOUSE SPARROW (top and bottom birds)

Dull, messy head colour

WINTER PLUMAGE MALE

WHERE FOUND
Widespread resident. Mostly marshland.

154

FLIGHT

Reed buntings have an undulating flight similar to yellowhammers. The white border to the tail is obvious when flying away. The tail is often flicked up and down on landing.

Tail flicked up and down

Long undulations in dipping flight

White tail borders

Some males have darker heads than others

Obvious white moustache

GARDEN TIPS

Reed buntings feed on seeds and crushed oats. They prefer to feed on the ground but will use bird-tables. Will visit gardens near marshy ground or commons and are most likely to be encountered in late winter.

SUMMER PLUMAGE MALE

VOICE

Only likely to be heard in the largest, wettest gardens, the reed bunting's song is very recognizable – a slow series of staccato notes, sounding like 'three… blind…mice'. Unpaired birds betray their status with faster songs of more notes.

NEST

Reed buntings build nests on or near the ground, most often in tussocks in wet areas. They raise two or three broods, each of four or five young. Recent research has shown that reed bunting society is rife with infidelity; females have many sexual liaisons outside the pair-bond and, if this happens, the male stops helping to feed the chicks.

155

Unusual garden birds

CANADA GOOSE
Branta canadensis, 90–100 cm (36–40 in).
A large goose, increasingly common all over our area. Most likely to be seen flying over suburban gardens. Distinguished from other geese by its black neck and white chin-strap, 'as if it had cut itself shaving'.

Black and white chin-strap

Crest in breeding plumage

Iridescent green plumage

Rounded wings

LAPWING
Vanellus vanellus, 29–32 cm (12 in).
Distinctive bird of farming areas. In hard weather, can be seen flying over almost anywhere. Colourful, with iridescent green and purple above, white below. Tumbles in display flight, shows off rounded wings. Has amazing shrill nasal cries, including 'pee-vit', which gives it the country name 'peewit'.

Heart-shaped face

Silent flight on rounded wings

BARN OWL
Tyto alba, 33–36 cm (13½ in).
Mostly nocturnal, appearing as a ghostly white apparition floating over the fields. Flies silently on rounded wings. Has unusual heart-shaped face. Takes to artificial nest-sites in buildings and trees, and makes blood-curdling scream.

Red
eyes

Long
wings

LONG-EARED OWL
Asio otus, 34–37 cm (14 in).
A nocturnal woodland owl; replaces tawny owl
in Ireland and some parts of the Continent.
Longer-winged than tawny in flight. Has red,
not black eyes. The ear-tufts are unique, but
not always easy to see. Young make begging
calls like a squeaky gate being opened.

Crest
raised
when
excited

Hovers in
display flight

SKYLARK
Alauda arvensis, 18–19 cm (7 in).
Seen fluttering over fields; often
hovers. Midway between sparrow
and starling in size. Shows white outer tail feathers, and white edges to
wings in flight. Runs over ground and often shows crest, especially when
excited. Has fantastic, outpouring song which never seems to stop.
Comes to feeding stations for grain in the winter. A very common
species all over our area.

Brown-
streaked
back

Streaked
breast

Long tail

Pink
legs

MEADOW PIPIT
Anthus pratensis, 14–15 cm (5¾ in).
'Small brown bird', looks like miniature thrush with pink legs and longish
tail with white outer tail feathers. No crest. Runs or walks on ground.
In 'parachute' display flight: rises, then descends with tail up and legs
down. Feeds at ground stations in the winter, mostly near farmland
or moorland.

Unusual garden birds

White breast

NIGHTINGALE
Luscinia megarhynchos, 16–17 cm (6½ in).
Justifiably famous for its rich and powerful
song, the nightingale *only* sings in spring,
mostly from April to June; birds heard at
night at other times are not nightingales
(often robins). Quite robin-like to look at,
but with white breast and long, prominent,
rufous tail. Shy and skulking in Britain,
often tame and very common on
Continent. Winters in Africa.

Long red tail

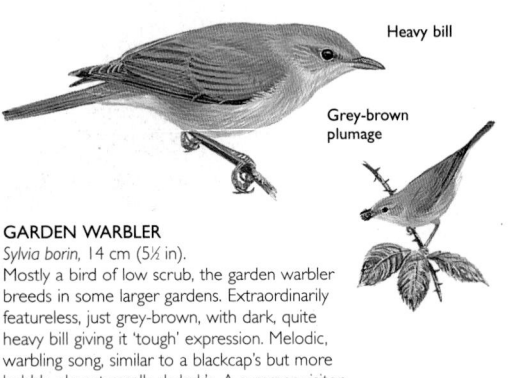

Heavy bill

Grey-brown plumage

GARDEN WARBLER
Sylvia borin, 14 cm (5½ in).
Mostly a bird of low scrub, the garden warbler
breeds in some larger gardens. Extraordinarily
featureless, just grey-brown, with dark, quite
heavy bill giving it 'tough' expression. Melodic,
warbling song, similar to a blackcap's but more
bubbly, almost recalls skylark's. A summer visitor.

Pale eye patch

SUMMER MALE

FEMALE

Silvery wing-bar

LINNET
Carduelis cannabina, 13–14 cm (5 in).
Small finch with confusing plumages.
Doesn't feed in trees like redpoll or
siskin, but more typically on ground
in fields and on farmland. Male in
summer unmistakable, otherwise
looks more grey-headed than female. Juveniles and females are more
streaky. All birds have pale patches around eyes, and silvery wing-bar.
Cheerful, hurried 'chup-chup' call. Resident and common. Sometimes
visits bird-tables for seeds.

Thin bill

White throat

Pink breast

Grey head

Brown wings

WHITETHROAT

Sylvia communis, 13–15 cm (5½ in).
A common, lively bird of scrub and
farmland. A warbler, with thin, insect-
eater's bill. Look for warm brown wings,
greyish head (noticeably peaked), and white
throat contrasting with pinkish breast. Male is much greyer than female.
Has perky, dancing song flight, accompanied by a fast, scratchy song.
Summer visitor, very common.

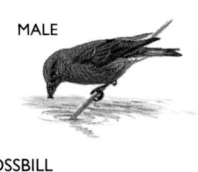

MALE

Crossed bill

FEMALE

No wing-bar

CROSSBILL

Loxia curvirostra, 16–17 cm (6½ in).
A finch that specialises in conifers, mostly
pine, spruce and larch – the latter in winter.
Large-headed and plump, male with brick-red
plumage, female green. Can resemble
greenfinch, but no wing-bars. Crossed
mandibles are a giveaway when visible.
Loud 'chip-chip' or 'jip-jip' call. Sometimes
comes to garden ponds in order to drink.

Huge, stout bill

Large head

Broad white wing-bar

HAWFINCH

Coccothraustes coccothraustes,
16–17 cm (6½ in).
Scarce and incredibly shy. Visits
gardens from neighbouring mature
woodland, especially if this contains
hornbeams. Large-headed, with
huge bill. With short tail, this gives
top-heavy profile, especially in
flight. Female is somewhat less
brightly coloured. Occasionally
visits bird-tables in early morning.

Index